RULES FOR ENGAGING GRIEF:
A PATH TO HEALING

RULES FOR ENGAGING GRIEF: A PATH TO HEALING

Terrence Douglas

Author of
Searching Sand Crabs in the Dark and *Ice Dance*

iUniverse, Inc.
New York   Lincoln   Shanghai

RULES FOR ENGAGING GRIEF: A PATH TO HEALING

iUniverse books may be ordered through booksellers or by contacting:

iUniverse
2021 Pine Lake Road, Suite 100
Lincoln, NE 68512
www.iuniverse.com
1-800-Authors (1-800-288-4677)

ISBN: 978-0-595-47414-1 (pbk)
ISBN: 978-0-595-71066-9 (cloth)
ISBN: 978-0-595-91692-4 (ebk)

Printed in the United States of America

In the beginning was the Word, and the Word was with God, and the Word was God, He was with God in the beginning.
—John 1:1-2[1]

For The Bringers of the Light—The Grandchildren

Andrew, Cade, Christopher, Caroline, Eliza, JD,
Keegan, Kelley, Lander, Liam, Michael, Zachary

Contents

Introduction

I lost Donna, my spouse of thirty-nine years, when a car struck her as she walked across the street holding my son Christopher's hand. They were on their way to his First Holy Reconciliation, a preparatory rite in the Catholic Church before he was to receive Holy Communion, days before Passion Sunday. They were sixty feet from the main entrance of the church.

I have written this book to share my journey in dealing with grief with those who have lost someone—spouse, child, parent, or friend—or suffered extreme grief prompted by some other circumstance, in the hope that some of what I learned will help to speed the reader's healing and return to emotional stability. Grief is a special journey all of its own.

Recently, I attended a fifty year high school reunion. One of my classmates announced the title of my recently published book of poetry—*Searching Sand Crabs in the Dark*[2], saying that not many former CIA case officers write poetry. Poetry is a way for me to access the deepest recesses of my heart. So in the pages that follow, in addition to the *Rules,* the reader will find my poetry.

Additionally, I have selected scripture readings and quotations that have proved valuable in my healing, and I hope they will be as helpful for the reader. Ignatius of Loyola, a sixteenth-century mystic and the founder of the Society of Jesus, or the Jesuit Order, commented that he had no one to turn to for guidance at the time of his conversion, so the Lord himself taught him the way a schoolteacher teaches a little child. Loyola once declared that even if all the scriptures were destroyed, he would hold on to what they revealed because of what the Lord had taught him.[3] I encourage the reader to become like a little child in listening to the voice within.

After each scripture or wisdom reading, I include a prayer, response, and reflection related to loss and rejection. As you will see, I have included the response that I received from the Holy Spirit, acknowledging that this may be the most powerful contribution to the *Rules.*

At the end of each Rule is an exercise. I suggest that the reader record and date his thoughts in special journal or in the blank pages that follow each Rule,

---

2   Douglas, Terry. *Searching Sand Crabs In The Dark: A Journey Inward.* New York, Lincoln, Shanghai: iUniverse, Inc. 2006

3   DeMello, Anthony. *The Song of the Bird.* New York: Image Books. 1982, p.171.

and review them every couple of months. I did this and was able to see remarkable progress in healing and reaching a place of further stillness.

Finally, I suggest that you do not attempt to read this book in one or two sessions. Allow the process of healing to extend over several weeks, picking up the book to consider each of the Rules at your own pace.

Terry Douglas
Sandbridge, Virginia
August 8, 2007

In Memoriam

I wrote the following poem in West Virginia on the first anniversary of Donna's death. Later in this volume, I explain how time began to lose its "timeliness," in that it was difficult to believe that my friend had departed a year earlier.

Cherry Blossoms

The cherry blossoms
Coming into bloom
Remind me
That one year has passed
Since you departed
From our view.

I remember last year,
Just after your passing,
How sad I felt to think
That you had just missed
The blossoms—
After the harsh winter snows.

Perhaps in my sorrow—
Too soon to see the meaning—
I missed them
As a sign for us
To celebrate your transition
To the Light.

This year in joy the blossoms
Remind me of your presence
Just below the surface
Of words, time, and events—
Of love rising in union,
A resurrection of sorts.

PART ONE

THE STORY

Early Years

Who would have imagined that the ten-year-old playing stickball on the streets of New York, where sewer covers marked the bases, would one day travel throughout the world and have the opportunity in later life to reflect upon those experiences? Well, I did.

I spent the first twenty years of my life in one of two brick walk-up apartment buildings of five stories each, separated by four city blocks. I lived with my mother, father, and sister—four years my junior—in a four-room apartment until we moved into a five-room apartment in the same building—three small bedrooms, a kitchen, and a family room. Iron fire escapes painted dark red hung across the front of the building. When I forgot my key, I leaped from the ground to grasp the lower rung, then scrambled to the top floor to gain access to our apartment through an unlocked window.

One early memory of childhood is walking along the Harlem River with my father when I was recovering from the whooping cough. It seems back then the air along the river—hardly pristine—held some medicinal value.

I did not see much of my father while I was growing up. He worked the night shift in the General Post Office in the city and held a second part-time job for thirty years. Every day, he left for work at 11 PM, returning the next afternoon. My mother worked as a waitress in Schrafft's, an upscale chain of restaurants scattered throughout the city. Both my parents rode the subway into the city. My father had it timed so that when he turned the corner he would often jog to the station five blocks distant so as not to miss the train.

I walked to Public School 86 for my elementary education. Three memories stand out for those years. The first concerns an incident on the first day of kindergarten. My grandmother was called in by the teacher because I put clay on the seat of the pretty girl sitting next to me, spoiling her dress. The second is when I was pitching for our softball team and threw away what would have been the final out in a championship game. The third is about two devoted teachers, Mr. Sheridan and Miss Jordan, who tutored me after school on subjects, not covered in the public school curriculum, that I would meet on the entrance exam for Fordham Preparatory.

It was my mother's undying determination to settle for nothing but to see her son educated at Fordham that set those wheels in motion. And, yes, I passed the entrance exam to this Jesuit high school, located on Fordham University's Rose Hill Campus about a thirty minute walk from my home. I remember the mailman, Mr. Packman, handing me the very thin envelope before he distributed the mail into the slots for the building. I opened the envelope, expecting the worst, and I remember my joy when I read the acceptance to the class of 1956. (Incidentally, my mother never doubted that I would pass the entrance exam. That says something about mothers!) The tuition for the year was less than five hundred dollars. My parents arranged to pay each month to lessen the burden on the family finances.

Those high school years filled me with a thirst for knowledge. The world opened for me as I read Caesar's *Gallic Wars* in Latin, Homer and the Battle of Salamis in Classical Greek, mythology that set aflame my imagination, and literature that encouraged me to distinguish the traits of a hero or main character as well as the flaws that give one breadth. There, too, I learned about a spiritual dimension that led me for the first time to consider my relationship with God. I attended two religious retreats of three days each when our class was bused to a rustic former inn in Monroe, New York. There I experienced first-hand meditation and contemplation—stillness—in short, profound prayer.

However, so that you do not think that I was too obedient for my age, let me recount an incident when I was thirteen years old. Three friends—Billy, Patty, Tommy—and I decided to enter the burned-out remains of a neighborhood bar and grill. Our route took us along a darkened alley to an outdoor staircase that led to an entrance on the second floor of the bar. We were on the hunt for any contraband that had survived the conflagration. We were inside for about thirty minutes and then reassembled on the roof with our loot—a large bundle of waterlogged napkins, a champagne bottle with its label seared off, and a damaged meat cutter. Patty looked off the roof and reported police cars parked askew on the main street. We hurried to the staircase to escape, but noticed flash light beams moving up the alley.

In panic, Billy and I decided to find an alternate escape route. We rushed to the edge of the roof on a side street. He grabbed a hold of the ledge, positioned himself, and let go, landing safely on the ground. As I took my place on the ledge, the molding collapsed and I fell, grazing my left hand on a spike fence and breaking my right arm upon landing. I can still hear my shouting in shock, "My leg! My leg!" and no mention of my arm, as we fled and I outdistanced Patty with my speed. When the police visited my home—(Tommy told the police our names)—they learned that I was in the hospital having my arm set and that my mother was very upset with me. Clearly, I had learned my lesson.

In my last year of high school I traveled by subway for forty minutes into the city to a Schrafft's store where I was a delivery boy. From the subway station, I walked past the Soviet Consulate on Park Avenue, unaware that some day I would be stealing secrets from the Soviets as a CIA intelligence officer stationed abroad. My special memory of that time was of an African-American lady who, when I appeared at the doorway, would toast a large corn muffin in the oven for me.

College and Further

I took the path of least resistance and applied for Fordham College upon graduation from the Prep. I ran for office in my freshman year, was elected, and fifty years later, I am still in contact with the rest of the winning slate. Though not much of an athlete in high school, I became an avid member of Fordham lightweight rowing team in my freshmen year, graduating to heavyweight varsity in my sophomore year. I devoted untold hours to rowing at dawn and sunset and competing for the university and, during the summer, with the New York Athletic Club. (I still race in my mind as I row a Concept2 indoor machine that I set up in my bedroom.)

As an English literature major, I aspired to write the great American novel—and still do. I focused on Ernest Hemingway's writing and still recall an adjunct professor—a former accountant—who inspired me. On the first day of class, he handed out a paragraph that Hemingway had written about the sunrise. The author's words still ignite me when I view a sunrise. I also studied Russian language at college. It was a new program and I decided to enroll so that I did not have to continue a mandatory second year of Classical Greek—after all, I reasoned, the Greek alphabet was the basis of the Cyrillic alphabet used in Russian, easing my transition to Russian.

Following college, I—like so many other graduates—entered law school. However, my experience was less than positive—I attribute my inability to maintain a 70 percent average to the very attractive young lady who sat alongside me in class. She was the distraction that I might have needed to realize that serving on the Supreme Court required more of this twenty-one year old than simply aging.

With the Berlin Crisis under way and the selective service draft looming, I enrolled in a graduate program in Russian Studies at Fordham. After I paid the last six hundred dollars from my bank account, I encountered Tim Healey, the former moderator of the rowing team, who was later to become the president of Georgetown University. When I told him the sad tale of my law school experience, he made an offer I could not refuse—become a resident administrator in his dormitory and earn a full fellowship that included all tuition in my pursuit of a master's degree, plus room and board. When my excitement calmed, I settled into a quiet prayer of thanksgiving.

Career and Marriage

Armed with an MA degree, I interviewed and was tested and later accepted by the Central Intelligence Agency, but first I had to enter the United States Air Force to fulfill my military service obligation. I was sent for three months to officer training school at Lackland Air Force Base in Texas. Upon commissioning, I was informed before my graduating class that I was assigned to Glasgow. I assumed I was on my way to Scotland, but before I showed any signs of gloating, I heard *Montana*—Glasgow, Montana, home to a B-52 bomber base. So from a city of eleven million, I reported to Glasgow AFB, seventeen miles north of a city of five thousand, where I was assigned to a combat defense squadron.

We can all point to an event or a time in our lives that served to alter irretrievably who we are or were to become. Being assigned to Glasgow and later being sent to Fairchild AFB in Spokane, Washington, on temporary duty were two interlinking coincidences—and we all know there are no coincidences. Just so you see how God works for the good in bringing me to Donna, let me set the stage in the following sequence of events.

Two young airmen from Glasgow were playing quick-draw on a flight line of nuclear-armed B-52s that were temporarily positioned at Fairchild while the Glasgow runway was being repaved. One of the sidearms discharged, striking the other guard in the shoulder; immediately there was a call for more officer supervision. A married lieutenant, my colleague in Glasgow, asked for a deferment; next in line, I accepted the assignment. I took out a $600 loan to replace my vehicle, which was in a repair shop, and left that afternoon. It is to be noted that I met Donna one week after I arrived in Spokane, proposed to her the next week, and we married within two months. Sometimes those coincidences are difficult to explain rationally.

Our first date was a double date with her roommate and Joe, a fellow officer who was to become my best man. Joe and I were newly arrived officers on TDY, that is, temporary duty. He was having difficulty meeting someone with whom to spend time. I provided him with Donna's number, but every time he called, no one answered. Impatient, I asked him to give me back the number and I called. To our surprise, she answered. (I learned later that she had been unavailable earlier because she was bidding goodbye to her fiancé who had left for Europe earlier in the day.) I spoke for Joe when I suggested that we meet.

Donna invited us both to dinner. She taught art in the Spokane school system. I agreed to go out with her roommate, who was a nurse at a local hospital.

Joe and I arrived on time, bringing with us a bottle of wine and bacon to wrap the steaks that Donna grilled on a hibachi. After dinner, I dutifully walked her roommate to the hospital. When I returned, Joe was dozing on the couch. I helped Donna clean up, and over dishes I discovered an attraction to her that Joe had not experienced. We made arrangements to search for petroglyphs[4] along the Columbia River two days later, once I completed a twenty-four stint as the duty officer of the base.

I remember how sleep-deprived I was when I arrived that morning to pick her up. In a sense, she picked me up because we drove her black 1963 Triumph-3 sports car and left behind my pale green 1956 four-door Ford sedan—the car I had purchased ten days earlier with a signature loan from the credit union.

Without adequate sleep, my peripheral vision seemed impaired and I feared I might tumble from the narrow path into the river. What an impression to make on a first date! However, when we finally settled at our picnic site, my fatigue lifted, it seems, because I remember lowering a bottle of Chianti on a long string into the river to cool.

A week later, I proposed marriage to her. Donna never found it very funny when I told the children that when I said *yes* to her proposal, I thought she was inviting me to see the original *Pink Panther* movie starring Peter Sellers, not proposing marriage. We married within two months of our meeting, but not before we took a short trip to Glasgow AFB. I wanted her to experience the heat of the summer firsthand and take my word for the severe winters.

In the rush to marriage, I only flinched once. I asked Donna if it seemed that we were moving too quickly. She agreed and suggested that we wait a year or so. In the interim, she planned to accept an offer to become an airline stewardess. That response prompted me to remain resolute and we married according to our original plan. I sometimes wonder how I would have responded had she been more anxious. Her calming personality, independence, and spark were traits that I valued so much in my love for her, and they remain close in my heart today.

Within the year after our marriage, our first daughter was conceived and we were driving to the East Coast. I was to begin training as a CIA operations, or case officer, learning to spot, recruit, and manage securely someone who had access to intelligence of value to United States national security, and honing writing and reporting skills. In the last phase of training, with the Viet Nam war

---

4   Indian stone carvings along the cliffs overlooking the river.

escalating, all of us in training learned that if we wanted to go further we would have to complete a paramilitary course previously reserved for volunteers.

The secret to avoid assignment as a team leader observing traffic on the Ho Chi Minh trail in Viet Nam was to maintain a position in the middle of the class. Those finishing with the highest grades would be sent to Viet Nam immediately upon graduation; those at the bottom of the class risked being fired. My success in staying in the middle was once threatened when I learned from a sympathetic instructor that I did quite well in an ambush exercise—I wondered if growing up in New York contributed to my prowess. The instructor intended to question the less than perfect grades for the other modules. I dissuaded him.

In addition to the *normal* curriculum for paramilitary training that included firearms and explosives training, we could volunteer for parachute or jump training. Almost without exception, our whole class of non-volunteers volunteered. Five jumps and I can remember each one. One of my classmates took a photograph of me sitting on a C-47 aircraft waiting for the commands to "Get ready, stand up, hook up, turn to the door, move to the door, jump." I cannot believe the tension lines that spread over my face prior to that first jump. That process is a perfect metaphor for life, as we move to the door and wait to see as we hurtle through space whether the parachute will open as our faith teaches. At the completion of training, I was assigned to the area division responsible for gathering intelligence on the hostile intentions of the Soviet Union.

Family and Espionage

Our first daughter was born at Walter Reed Hospital. Donna went into labor on Friday afternoon and we had to drive around the Beltway from Alexandria, Virginia, to the hospital in the District of Columbia. In retrospect, there was no reason to fear that I would be assisting the birth in bumper-to-bumper traffic. Donna was in labor for twenty-two hours. She gave birth minutes after I left the waiting room—two straight-back chairs at the top of a staircase with a ten-year old *Sports Illustrated* to memorize—to have a hamburger and a beer. When I returned and spoke to her in the recovery room, she asked if I had been drinking!

While we are on coincidences, I was assigned to Warsaw because I showed up for work at CIA Headquarters on a snow day. I was one of the few young officers at work that day and when the head of personnel walked past my cubicle and saw me, he returned to ask me to come to his office. There he confirmed that I spoke Russian and was willing to study Polish and accept an assignment to the embassy in Warsaw. Within days, I began one-on-one Polish language training in preparation.

We set sail from New York on the *S.S. United States* with our expanding family of two daughters. Our destination was Le Havre, France. However, General de Gaulle, the president of the French Republic, was facing an almost total shutdown of the nation in response to the crisis in Algeria, a former French colony that de Gaulle supported for independence. So we disembarked in Bremerhaven, Germany, after a short stop in Southampton, England. We were ready to board a train for Frankfurt with our children, eleven pieces of luggage, a white German shepherd dog, a Siamese cat, very little cash, no German language skills, and no reservations, but with much laughter and adventurous spirits.

We survived the journey and I began my first assignment in espionage. Donna taught in the American School in Warsaw, our older daughter began preschool, and we grew closer in love. We made friends that to this day occupy a special place in my heart and celebration of life. We attended a local Polish church—more a chapel—and befriended the Polish priests, one of whom was going blind because the necessary medicine was not available in the hard currency pharmacy maintained for the elite. Through a recently acquired contact in Frankfurt, I managed to have the proper medicine sent to me in a diplomatic pouch. In reciprocation, these young priests arranged to have Donna confirmed in the Catholic rite by Cardinal Wyszynski, then the ruling prelate of Poland. He would later have been a leading candidate to become Pope had he not been diagnosed with a terminal illness.

By then our third daughter was born and I expected to remain a *damski kraviec*, Polish for *female tailor*, a term assigned to fathers who only had daughters. Incidentally, it's not an especially pejorative expression because it also implies that such a father had a way with women. What man would renounce this title? Before Donna returned from giving birth in the United States, I remember arranging with the housing staff to have a new double bed sent in to replace the two singles pulled together that served us until then.

Lest I be accused only of selecting bedroom furniture during this tour, let me describe one of several experiences when a rush of adrenalin punctuated our lives there. Donna and I and our third daughter—three months old—drifted off into Old Town Warsaw, ostensibly to go shopping, on a Friday evening. Actually, we were checking for surveillance from the Polish security service. When we confirmed that we were *clean*, we drove outside Warsaw to establish contact with someone who had indicated previously an interest in cooperating with us. Donna was with me so as not to alarm the security service, and our daughter came along because Donna was still breast-feeding her and could not be separated from her in the event we were arrested.

I parked on the outskirts of the small town and left Donna and our daughter with her. I can still hear the frogs croaking as I walked to the residence of the volunteer. All went well, and as I was walking back to the car, I spotted about one hundred yards distant a police vehicle turning at high speed toward me. I dismissed any notion of trying to elude the police and continued to walk, hunkered down so as not to draw attention to my height. The police stopped thirty feet in front of me, exited the car with automatic weapons, and proceeded to run directly at me. At the last minute, they veered off into an apartment building on the left. I expelled the air slowly from my lungs and continued at the same pace to my vehicle with Donna and our newborn. We returned with no further incident. I have often thought of the missed opportunity for both policemen had they stopped the errant spy on a mission far from where one would expect him to be.

From Warsaw we were assigned directly to Delhi—with some relief. Why? I had filled out the reassignment questionnaire—or dream sheet, as we called it—and had requested a Spanish-speaking area, Montevideo, as my first choice of three alternatives. Days after I forwarded the request to Washington, the

Tupamaros, a homegrown Uruguayan terrorist group, began kidnapping foreign diplomats. I had expected that Washington, under the circumstances, would honor my request.

I was thankful for the Delhi assignment because that is where Donna and I enjoyed time with our three children. They were soon to be joined by a son whom we named for a missionary we befriended there, and later by a little girl whom we adopted from Mother Theresa's orphanage in Delhi. Donna met the little girl on her weekly trips to the orphanage until the day she was in isolation due to the staph infection she had contracted. Donna asked that we take her to an embassy doctor for treatment, and on the ride back to the orphanage we decided to adopt her. Donna and I did not take much time reaching agreement on important matters.

We went horseback riding as a family almost daily. Once when Donna was six months pregnant with our son, I noticed, through the embassy office window of a colleague, Donna cantering down the path. I was thankful that our son's head has not shown any creases from those prenatal rides. We played tennis, swam at the embassy club, and took the children on picnics. I can still see Donna taking tennis lessons, determined as she was to be competitive. There we both learned how to let go of time considerations, and be present. The weather was glorious—aside from a few months of dry heat and the monsoon. Donna managed a staff of servants, headed up by a Kasai woman from Assam, and used to say that without servants she would never have considered caring for five children.

And yes, I also worked in India. The Soviets had signed a friendship treaty with the government of India and I was one of several intelligence officers assigned to obtain information on the ramifications of this agreement. We experienced a short-term Indo-Pak war. During the blackout, I was jogging on the street toward the embassy with the first intelligence report following the outbreak of the war. A young Indian on a bicycle asked if I wanted a ride. I accepted but suggested—due to my height and weight—that I pedal and he ride behind me. He agreed and that is how I reached the American embassy compound.

Donna also was involved in the business of espionage. Regularly, she would accept a package wrapped in a Kashmiri shawl passed furtively to her by a sensitive agent in a shop. The Indian security service did not place women under surveillance—who would entrust them with state secrets? Thus, in those years, Donna accumulated many Kashmiri shawls for her service.

I had learned a year before that I would next be assigned to Beirut. At the time, my friends indicated their jealousy of my good fortune. However, when we arrived a year later, even my *enemies* felt sorry for me. The civil war had erupted and months later, Donna and the children were evacuated to Athens. There, they all lived in a two-room apartment, together with our nanny from the Seychelles. During our separation, I wrote to Donna daily and brought the letters to the evacuation point for onward delivery to the American embassy in Athens. Though apart, our love relationship deepened and matured.

At this time, my professional focus included counter-terrorism, as I gathered intelligence on terrorist-related groups that were fomenting strife and violence throughout the Middle East and Europe. My dark humor from my days in New York improved as I sought to reduce the stress irrational violence precipitated.

I, like so many of my colleagues, did not enjoy the family separation. The first opportunity I had to see Donna and the children was just after Christmas when I was allowed to leave Beirut for a few days. On my day of departure, an outburst of fighting delayed our flight for a couple of hours. I was so pleased to see Donna waiting for me at the airport in Athens. She had managed to retrieve our vehicle from the storage area in Piraeus, the seaport where our shipment had arrived from India.

Dismissing my offer to drive, she took the wheel and drove as a veteran through the streets of Athens to the Hilton Hotel. Instead of seeing the children first, Donna made arrangements for us to have some time alone. After our tryst, I remember seeing a young newly married case officer from Beirut in the coffee shop eating ice cream with his bride, and thinking to myself that I preferred our priorities. Of course most probably that was their priority as well.

During this short stay in Athens, a senior CIA official flew in from Washington to ask me to volunteer for a mission to locate a notorious international terrorist. I agreed without hesitation. When I told Donna later of my decision, tears formed in her eyes. It was only one of four or five times that I saw Donna cry in all our years together. Later she agreed that accepting the mission was the right thing to do She supported me fully and remained in Athens with the children while I traveled throughout Europe, going from one capital to the next to try to penetrate various terrorist cells.

Without Washington's awareness, I arranged a few times for Donna to meet me for a weekend when I expected to be in one place for more than a few days. Our nanny cared for the children in her absence. We financed these brief encounters with the money I saved from my *per diem*—the money I received for each day apart from my family.

By spring of that year, I expected that we would be sent back to Washington. We had been abroad for eight years. We were looking forward to settling into the new house we had purchased while abroad and had yet to occupy. And then a message came. I was asked to serve in Berlin. Donna loved life abroad and with little discussion about the pros and cons of such an assignment, we accepted and made arrangements to ship our household goods to Berlin while we enjoyed two months in the States visiting our families.

Over those years outside the United States, not only had our family grown, but it had grown closer together. Like a migrant clan, we moved as a unit across the globe, leaving relationships in our wake but viewing our family unit as critical to the stability we sought. During those years, Donna and I became closer as friends in a spiritual, emotional, and physical union.

Before we left the States for Berlin, our adopted daughter received expedited naturalization from the Department of Immigration and Naturalization Services. After a lifetime in New York, my parents had moved to Los Angeles, and when I appeared there for the initial immigration appointment, I realized that the experience would be memorable. The clerk asked me if the application was for me. I was not three-foot-six-inches, as stated on the first page of the form, and I gestured to the little girl accompanying me, whose head did not reach the countertop.

The interview with the director of the INS office had been arranged by the liaison officers in Washington. In the course of the interview, the director informed me rather gratuitously that he had never seen a birth certificate with the inoculation record on the back. While most interesting, he informed me, it would not be sufficient for the naturalization process. I told him that the little girl had been abandoned on the streets of Calcutta before reaching Mother Theresa's orphanage, which created the birth certificate and the inoculation record. I also reminded him that it was sufficient for an American visa and had allowed us to complete the adoption process. The bureaucrat would not budge. In my frustration, I told him that I would have someone call him from Washington. He smiled. I placed a collect call to my contact there and, in minutes, the repentant official called me back into his office and expedited the naturalization process.

Our stay in Berlin was distinguished by the Wall that still encircled the city. In my position we traveled regularly into East Berlin where there were several sites worth visiting—a zoological park that the children loved, an opera house whose performances were attended by the Allies attired in their colorful dress uniforms, and a small private restaurant that thrived despite the colorless Communist economy. We lived in a huge pre-war house that had a round dining room with a round table that could seat twenty guests when the wooden slats were extended. In the basement, a bomb shelter, secured by a revolving steel wheel similar to that found on a submarine, provided living quarters for our nanny. I used to muse about when the previous owner decided that it was time to build the bomb shelter.

Though the Second World War had ended over thirty years ago, the city was still divided into the Soviet, French, British, and American sectors. Among the benefits of serving in Berlin at that time were French wine for fifty cents per liter; a free overnight train to Strasbourg or Frankfurt; attendance at the changing of the guard ceremony at Spandau Prison, where Rudolph Hess was confined, and, after the ceremony unlimited quantities of Russian crab and vodka; sailing on the Wannsee; and simply walking in the Grunewald—a forest of trees, most of which were planted after the Second World War to replace those cut down for fuel during the harsh winters of 1943-1944 and 1946-1947—close to our residence.

In Berlin Donna joined the staff of the Red Cross and received more calls than I in the middle of the night. Hers were related to family emergencies requiring emergency travel orders for military assigned there. We became closely involved in the Christian community in Berlin and befriended the military chaplains. The senior chaplain, a U.S. Army colonel, once insisted that I give the talk for the upcoming prayer breakfast and he would not accept *no* for my answer. All turned out fine when I let go—a lesson I have taken to heart these many years—and accepted the real possibility that my presentation would be a professional disaster. The title, "Prayer for Us Overachievers," came to me almost on a divine breath and the talk had an impact I had not anticipated.

Donna was truly gifted in asking the most penetrating question of my Soviet-Bloc targets in the most disarming manner. Whenever we were to host a foreign intelligence official, I would tell her the information that I was hoping to obtain. For example, we suspected a certain Polish official as an intelligence officer of some interest, but the photograph on file did not conclusively identify him as the man sought. In course of the evening, Donna posed several questions that served to identify him conclusively. Had I posed the questions, I would have aroused unnecessary suspicion.

On two separate occasions during our time in Berlin, we vacationed in Majorca. A Jesuit missionary whom we had befriended in India made arrangements according to Donna's instructions: "Please find a quiet place on a crowded beach." The missionary was born in Majorca and, while on vacation there, he drove around the island on his motor scooter until he located what Donna sought—a quiet condominium on a beautiful beach.

Moving On

It is easy to segment life according to foreign assignments. When we returned finally to the States after eleven years abroad, the years do not group as easily. Soon after our return, I resigned from CIA. I came to the conclusion that life in the clandestine service—as the operations directorate was named—would not be the mind-expanding experience I sought at this point in my life. I would continue to recruit agents and *run* them securely. Leaving the agency was like leaving the priesthood. It took years for me to recover from missing the company of such talented individuals. A couple of years later, a suicide bomber destroyed the former hotel that housed the U.S. Embassy in Beirut. When people continued to badger me about whether I regretted my decision to resign, I responded: "Not if I would have been in the Embassy when it was blown up." That statement usually cut off further questions.

For the next ten years I was involved in developing plans to ensure that the leadership in the nation could continue to fulfill its responsibility in the event of war. The term used to describe such activity was *continuity of government operations* and at the time it was treated as a most sensitive subject. Donna, for her part, found employment with a defense company that supported such planning. She dutifully received the same security clearance that I had. I still smile when I think of her revealing to the program's security officer who was administering the indoctrination that I was her husband. He was struck dumb and wondered if there was some sort of security breach by having both husband and wife in the same program. That was not the case.

In her free time between a full time job and raising five children, Donna became an auxiliary police officer in the county where we resided. One of many incidents with which she would regale family gatherings was when she got hung up—literally—climbing over a fence as she responded to a possible burglary. Her partner entered the building through the front door. Only her shouts brought his assistance, and she required a ride home to change uniforms.

At the age of forty-six, she entered the police academy. I fully supported her decision, though we both discussed what she would do when she got lost in a police cruiser, since Donna had a terrible sense of direction. Though she passed the academic portion of the academy, she was washed out when she failed the night pursuit driver training conducted on a Formula One track in West Virginia. This was only the second time I ever saw Donna cry.

From working in continuity of government, I joined a Saudi-owned company of which I later became president. We provided security instruction to the Saudi military and protection to members of the royal family when they traveled abroad. In the course of two years I flew to and from Jeddah twelve times, remaining in the kingdom for an average of two weeks.

On one occasion, a Saudi general liaison officer drove our team up to a military facility in Taif at an elevation of three thousand feet. A treacherous two-lane road hugs the hills as it climbs higher and higher. It is said that Shaikh Mohammed bin Awad bin Laden, a camel driver from Yemen, offered to build the road when all of the engineers told King Abdul Azziz, the founder of Saudi Arabia, that it could not be done. On this success, bin Laden not only established a far reaching engineering and construction firm but also sired Osama bin Laden of Al Qaeda fame, one of thirty-three sons. In Taif, I was presented with a copy of the Koran, translated into English and printed in Maryland, by a young Saudi parachute lieutenant with whom I had discussed this holy book.

Donna visited the kingdom when I had taken ill and was hospitalized in Jeddah. She flew over and during the stay had an opportunity to shop in the old *souk*, or marketplace. When she returned to the hospital, she was wearing the head-to-floor black grown worn by Saudis to avoid the attention of the religious police who customarily cane women who bare their elbows or ankles. I was surprised that she had decided to conform and asked her about her decision. Just as quickly she said that she did not want anything to interfere with her shopping. Yes, Donna could be a woman of compromise, if required.

The Saudi prince eventually decided to dissolve the company that I headed—it was rumored that he expected to replace his half-brother as ambassador to the United States. Just before his decision, Donna and I had purchased a condominium in Virginia Beach. For seven years, we drove to our beach home each weekend to escape the frenetic pace of northern Virginia. We dined, hosted dinner parties, walked the beach, kayaked, and read. Donna was not a big supporter of athletic activity and in our double kayak she would often sit at ease in the stern as I rowed. Once, a voice called out from across the bay: "Hey, mister, the lady in the rear is not rowing!" Our trips became more complicated and finally ceased when my father came to live with us. At the same time, our adopted grandson began to attend school, limiting our travel flexibility.

As a surprise for Donna, I purchased a black Miata to remind her of the black TR-3 she had owned—or rather, that the credit union had owned—at the time of our marriage. My salary then, as a second lieutenant with less than two years of service, amounted to $222.22 per month. The monthly payment was more than we could afford.

After the Saudi adventure, I devoted my efforts to wide range of pursuits—if only I had determined earlier what I was going to be when I grew up! I supported clients who were seeking to invest abroad through due-diligence investigations, developed and conducted business war games to assist in the strategic planning process, represented foreign firms intent on business in the U.S., and followed many other pursuits as well.

It was during these years that Donna's vocation as a healer blossomed. She took courses in art therapy at a local university and sought to apply her excellent grades into a masters degree program, only to be denied the opportunity after a review of her undergraduate transcript from over twenty years earlier. Momentarily deterred, she became a certified practitioner in Guided Imagery and Music[5] and worked for years in a school for emotionally disturbed children. She complemented her healing qualities with training in *reiki,*[6] *feng shui,*[7] and *shamanism.*[8] Her extraordinary gift was to reach all people from the heart so gently, helping those in need to heal the trauma that sometimes lurked just beneath the surface.

Life was not all work, though; we vacationed in Hawaii several times. There, we rose each day before dawn to witness another sunrise, savoring coffee with sweetened milk. This was a holiday treat we had first experienced in Greece.

We also traveled to Egypt with a group led by a Maori medicine man. Donna suffered a serious bout of food poisoning during a stop in Aqaba and remained on the bus while I trekked up to the summit of Mount Sinai, past St. Catherine's Monastery. At the top, I left the group to jog back to Donna, who was on an air mattress on the floor of the bus. On the ride back into the hotel, I reached down to comfort her by holding her hand, only to discover later that the hand I was holding belonged to another lady who kept squeezing my hand in return. So much for attending to my ill wife!

We went scuba diving in Cancun and, from the Bahamas, we swam with wild dolphins beyond the Gulf Stream. In Bermuda we parasailed, almost reaching the clouds, or at least, with my acrophobia, that is what I feared might happen!

---

5   This is a healing process developed by Helen Bonny. For more information, see http://www.bonnyfoundation.org/intro.html.

6   For information on this healing process, see http://en.wikipedia.org/wiki/Reiki.

7   See http://en.wikipedia.org/wiki/Feng_Shui for explanatory notes.

8   Donna studied with Michael Harner who established the institute mentioned in the following: http://www.shamanism.org/

It is sometimes difficult to take in the full panorama of life, if we limit ourselves to a linear perspective and do not experience the full dimension of life measured in love relationships. During these years Donna and I witnessed three college graduations and four weddings as our children embarked on their own paths—so different from ours. Our family expanded with the birth of ten grandchildren—one of whom we adopted and reared.

In between assignments, prompted by Donna's passion to study, I accompanied her to workshops devoted to cross cultural healing. I was invariably one of a few males in attendance. We went out on dates weekly and changed our pattern to luncheons when we became responsible for our grandchild. Since he attended school during the day, we were free to frolic.

Donna never wandered too far from her great talent as an artist. As a surprise birthday present, she painted an oil of my last rowing regatta. The painting, taken from a photograph of the event, portrayed the two racing shells heading for the finish line with my team in front.

And Then

And then there was that life-changing event. I had just returned from a trip where I facilitated a three-day business war game for a corporate client in the midst of a strategic planning cycle. When I returned, Donna asked if I was open to a picnic in the mountains of West Virginia. Almost as an afterthought, she said that a real estate agent was going to show us some property that had just been opened for sale. We viewed a thirty-two acre tract at the top of the mountain and were so attracted to the 360-degree panorama that we purchased the land on the spot.

Not long thereafter, I accepted the position of academic department chair for an online university with newly established headquarters in Charles Town, West Virginia—some fifteen miles from the top of our mountain. Our plans to build a home on the property accelerated and almost before we realized it, we sold our home of twenty-five years. We purchased an interim home in West Virginia, close to building site, and enrolled our son in a private elementary school in the area. Donna devoted her energy and talent to the design of the mountain abode.

Heavy equipment was moved onto the mountain to clear the property and four days before the work was to commence, Donna was killed as she walked with Christopher in a crosswalk to church where he was to experience a church initiation prior to receiving First Holy Communion. The driver of the vehicle was looking to the right instead of to the left where pedestrians were crossing the street that he was entering.

> *And then one or other dies. And we think of this as love cut short; like a dance stopped in mid career or a flower with its head unluckily snapped off—something truncated and therefore, lacking its due shape. I wonder. If, as I can't help suspecting, the dead also feel the pains of separation ... [T]hen for both lovers, and for all pairs of lovers without exception, bereavement is a universal and integral part of our experience of love. It follows marriage as normally as marriage follows courtship or as autumn follows summer. It is not a truncation of the process but one of its phases; not the interruption of the dance, but the next figure. We are "taken out of our self"*

by the loved one while she is here. Then comes the tragic figure of
the dance in which we must learn to be still taken out of ourselves
though the bodily presence is withdrawn, to love the very Her, and
not fall back to loving our past, or our memory, or our sorrow, or
our relief from sorrow, or own love.[9]

In our span of time together, we lived throughout the world on assignment for the CIA—Poland, India, Lebanon, Greece, and Germany, and traveled elsewhere on vacation—Egypt, Mexico, Greece, Spain, Malaysia, Great Britain, and so many other countries. We raised five children, experienced together the joy of ten grandchildren, and found an additional blessing in raising one of them: Christopher, whom we adopted as our son.

Donna and I loved, laughed, cried, explored, worked, studied, dreamed, prayed, forgave, and sought to understand the mystery of life and death. We were so fully engaged and committed that when she died there was nothing I *had* to say to her. We had said and lived it all during those treasured years.

Those who knew her could see that she was unusually gifted with a sense of freedom, compassion, love, humor, honesty, and so much more. Her departure—so sudden—left our children, grandchildren, family, and friends time to ponder anew the gift of life, love, and relationships, and to this day such reflection continues for me.

In the memorial homily for Donna, the retired Jesuit priest who celebrated the mass observed, "Saintly people come into our lives not just as a pleasant diversion, but by God's design. God wants them to be models for us, so that we might learn how to love better in the time remaining to us."

During the time since Donna's departure, I have thought about and prayed deeply over her passing. A year after her passing, I married an old friend of Donna's and mine. The marriage did not prosper and we divorced within the year. The following pages, therefore, contain the fruit of my journey as I search the deeper mysteries of love, separation, rejection—a new sting for me—renewal, and reunion. I had little experience in all these emotions, but they afforded the growth that followed.

The image that came to me early on in this journey was that of a rope bridge in the mountains of Tibet. (The closest I came to Tibet was during a trek to the base camp of Annapurna in western Nepal.) In my imagination, I could hear water coursing through a gorge far below. The wind howled as it buffeted the rope bridge that swayed ominously as I ventured onto it. Some of the wooden slats were missing, and those that remained clacked loudly in

---

9   Lewis, C.S. *A Grief Observed.* New York: Seabury Press, 1961, 41.

the wind howling through the mountain pass. I could not see where I was headed because the morning fog had not yet lifted.

I had a sense that my destination was a purposeful one and one that many on the cliff behind me were observing. Many more on the yet-obstructed terminus point were awaiting my arrival with anticipation. And there I was, holding tight to a guide rope too low for my height. My first steps were halting. I tried to slide forward one foot after the other. Soon I realized that however short or even tentative it was, I had to take a step. I could not look back to see my progress for fear of tumbling off this insecure, swaying platform.

That is where I was in those first days, weeks, and months. In retrospect, the rope bridge has come to represent my journey between grief, rejection, healing, and growing wisdom and insight to the hurting heart. Along the way I discovered an ancient truth—those who know deep grief gain an enormous capacity to experience joy and love, and, ultimately, counsel. Possibly that is why God allows it. I can only distinguish my life now as filled with deep laughter amid the occasional tear, as God completes this good work He has promised in me.

Donna is never far from our thoughts. On a recent Sunday at mass, Chris turned to me and whispered that God informed him that his mom was busy and couldn't talk to him, but if she could it would be to tell him that she loved him.

The following is the Native American prayer that Donna carried in her wallet:

> O' Great Spirit,
> Whose voice I hear in the winds,
> And whose breath gives life to all the world,
> Hear me! I am small and weak, I need your strength and wisdom.
> Let me walk in beauty, and make my eyes ever behold the red and purple sunset.
> Make my hands respect the things you have made and my ears, sharp to hear your voice.
> Make me wise so that I may understand the things you have taught my people.
> Let me learn the lessons you have hidden in every leaf and rock.
> I seek strength, not to be greater than my brother, but to fight my greatest enemy—myself.
> Make me always ready to come to you with clean hands and straight eyes.

So when life fades, as the fading sunset, my spirit may come to you without shame.

Donna, I am certain, came to her Maker with straight eyes and without shame.

A final truth for me is that there is no end to the journey. The reader's commitment to the healing process unfolds as a work in progress, as does mine.

PART TWO

THE APPLICATION

Rules for Engaging Grief

Soon after Donna's death, one of my daughters sent me a poem and suggested that I resume writing poetry to capture the deep emotions I was experiencing. This same daughter talked of the texture of our lives measured in our responses to life's joys and sufferings.

The following poem emerged soon thereafter. You might note that long before I met Donna, I spent many hours on the expansive waterways of Long Island Sound as a member of crew for Fordham University and the New York Athletic Club, where I rowed eights, fours with and without coxswain, and pairs with and without coxswain.[10] I can still hear so clearly the rap of the wooden chucks as the coxswain struck the gunnels in an attempt to revive us, the oarlocks clicking against them as the sixteen foot oars entered and exited the water, and the hiss of the whirlpool swirl formed by a powerful stroke. Hear the cadence in the poem as I take each stroke.

I Sought Love

I
Calm water
Crisp air
Early sun
Glow warm

Oars snap
Shell runs
Straight back
Breathe out

---

10 Rowing, or *crew*, is a sport that requires discipline, commitment, strength, and endurance. It is a team sport, but only rugged individuals need apply. Races are held far beyond the cheers of supporters on shore. The coxswain is a critical member of the team who cannot weigh less than one hundred and ten pounds. He/she must be an irascible individual who urges the crew to exceed what they imagined possible in a close race—sometimes by calling for a last twenty strokes when in reality forty strokes remain. That's one reason that coxswains are traditionally thrown into the water after a winning effort.

"Hear me.
I love You!"
"What is love?"
You ask.

II
Donna enters
Life churns
Vibrates
Excites
Connects

III
And as she passes on
In loneliness
I understand better
Love.
Love is
Let go
Trust
Sacrifice
Trust
Steadiness
Trust
Compassion
Trust
Gentleness
Trust
Giving
Trust
Reaching out
Trust
Forgiveness
Trust
Confidence
Trust
Joy
Trust
Acceptance

Trust
Patience
Trust
Dream
Trust
Eternal
Trust

IV
Calm water
Crisp air
Early sun
Glow warm
Oars snap
Shell runs
Straight back
Breathe out

"Hear me,
I love You!"
"I know."

Along with a deeper realization of love, the Rules contained herein, or the guidelines that follow, began to emerge for me as I *cleared the deck* to deal with the powerful grief I was experiencing. The Rules outline the lessons that I am learning as I confront grief and loss directly. The reader will discover that the Rules are modeled after the rules of engagement issued to military units to frame the authorized response to an enemy's actions. While it turns out that grief is not exactly the enemy it initially appears to be, grief does test one's fortitude, patience, even bravery. It reveals itself as the teacher who appears when the student is ready.

The first set of Rules focus on the immediate period after the loss when the suffering is acute. The later Rules apply more to dealing with the chronic pain endured. For most, this pain will dissipate but not disappear. Chronic emotional pain is similar to the chronic physical pain experienced from an old knee injury that remains for a lifetime. The Rules set the stage for recovery over the first months and the insights contained therein apply to easing the chronic pain as well.

You will find after each Rule a suggested exercise that is designed to stir your response to this healing process. Record your thoughts in the space provided. I also recommend that you highlight words that are significant to you while reading, realizing that healing has its own season. The depth and speed of your healing might be directly proportional to the thoroughness of your responses to this manual on addressing grief. So we begin with the first Rule. Once again, each Rule follows this format:

- Rule—for engaging your grief
- A scripture reference or occasional quote—to ponder
- Prayer/Question—from me to the Father
- Response—what I received from the Holy Spirit
- Reflection—my understanding of what I received
- Poem—relating to the theme expressed in the Rule
- Exercise—optional but highly recommended

RULES 1-6

Rule 1—Grief releases—as we are ready—the grip of the past and the anxieties about a future, stimulates—in retrospect—a passion to embrace a hurt from which to grow. And in their place, we experience the eternal in the present moment.

> *Now we see but a poor reflection as in a mirror; then we shall see face to face. Now I know in part; then I shall know fully, even as I am fully known.*[11]

Prayer—Lord, somehow in this time of loss and focused as I am on the present, I catch a glimmer of the eternal. Please help me to see with confidence what you are showing me right now.

Response—Imagine yourself flying in an open cockpit through thick clouds. Every minute or so you see that on the sea below you, a ship is plying its way across the open expanse, ripples forming at a 45 degree angle from the bow. As quickly, the clouds fold in and you are once again flying blind. Those brief openings allow you to gauge your position and altitude. In the clouds, time seems to slow as the motor groans loudly or more quietly as the dense clouds and wind from the propeller alter the sound.

Reflection—Your experience with time and its irrelevance in matters of the heart and in the grieving process are hints of the eternity that awaits you as the clouds lift in your journey across the ocean. In this time, simply suspend anxiety about what you could have done in the past or should do in the future, and remain in the present. Focus intently on the words that you receive and experience gently the parting of the veil.

Many years ago I hurried along the footpath beside the Rhine River near Bad Godesberg, Germany. At that time the U.S. Embassy was located there, before it was transferred to Berlin. I was in Germany to "handle"—in the jargon of espionage—an agent, who was providing intelligence on the emerging international terrorist threat. My rush along the Rhine though had nothing to do with espionage. I was hoping to hear Corrie ten Boom's presentation at a

---

11   1 Corinthians 13:12

31

local church. Corrie was then in her eighties. Her book, *The Hiding Place*,[12] is a remarkable spiritual journal describing how her family hid a Jewish family from the Nazis who occupied her native Holland during World War II.

Having walked this path many times, I knew that there was no way that I would reach the lecture in time, so I settled into an easy, almost altered pace, letting go of any anxiety about entering the hall late. To my surprise, I arrived with minutes to spare and Corrie began her talk on time. Until this day that memory has stayed with me. It was then I first recall the experience of linear time evaporating into timelessness.

Nine months after Donna's passing I first realized that time had lost its significance. If someone had asked if she died last week, or three years ago, it would have been difficult to explain how it did not matter. Since it did not matter, I was puzzled by the question of time. Her death had passed into another dimension, free of time's boundaries, like the *kronos* and *kairos* of classical Greek.[13]

Though the loss is not now as acute or raw, it is still vivid. As I reflected on this phenomenon, I began to see that the veil to eternity was parting. No longer was time a factor in forgetting something from the past or an asset to achieving something in the distant future. Instead, I found that I could part the curtain, could see through the glass, and could experience the joy of eternity. Indeed, God was helping me to see in the mirror and on the other side of the mirror more clearly, as he had promised in the referenced scripture above. Simply stated, I was growing in my grief.

---

12   ten Boom, Corrie and John Scherrill. *The Hiding Place*. Old Tappan, NJ: Bantam, 1971.

13   *Kronos* is chronological time, or linear time, with a past and present leading to an undefined future, whereas *kairos* is a measurement of time in the present. It is opportune or seasonable time, without any particularly fixed boundaries.

Until Forever

I will wait for you until forever—
My declaration of patience timeless in import.
A breakthrough that spans an eternity,
Rather eternities of Love without boundaries.

No-time, no-space, dimension-less body,
Births without lifetimes, a supra-consciousness,
Leaping and bounding within soul union
As fear, loss, and separation release.

Acknowledging an ever present moment
Alive in creative surrender made possible
Through heart-tears and brokenness that
Yields to an alchemic, even Divine, transformation.

Illumination—enlightenment confirms.
How healing to surrender
To the impulse of Divine Love
From which all Love emanates.

I will wait for you until forever.

Rule 1 Exercise—A Sufi asks the student, "Who were you before your mother and father were born?" What better question to plumb the timeless and spaceless dimension of eternity. This was the question that I asked a dear friend who was dying of cancer and sought consolation, seeking a confidence for which a successful career did not provide or prepare him.

Describe below an experience where time seemed to lose its hold on your attention. It might have been when an anticipated incident was unfolding, a moment of fear that seemed to last an eternity, or one that was over in an instant. The purpose of this exercise is to break the bounds of time, the control the watch on your wrist holds, by demonstrating its insignificance in the wake of the truly memorable moments—good, frightening, or deliriously joyful—in your life. Think, remember, and express yourself now. If you are still not sure how to begin, imagine you were talking or sharing your thoughts with the Creator.

My Thoughts

My Thoughts

My Thoughts

Rule 2—You must let yourself heal. Healing comes—you can't command it, and no one can do it for you. Time does not exist in this process and it is possible the *sting* will bite again when you least expect it—thinking you are healed.

> *The centurion replied: Lord, I do not deserve to have you come under my roof. But just say the word, and my servant will be healed.*[14]

Prayer—Lord, help me to distinguish my need to accept responsibility for my healing and these words of scripture.

Response—In dealing with grief and loss you are all centurions, responsible for trudging along the path for the assistance you require and not remaining motionless in self-pity. Self-pity is distinguished by its hopelessness, while seeking help and believing that it will be provided is a rich sign of faith. So to your question, Mathew's words are an invitation to seek the healing grace for yourself and others. It was the centurion's grief over his servant's illness that spurred him into action—inquiring about Jesus, determining his location, and then seeking him out—and yours to heal your grief and that of your family and friends.

Reflection—Despite the enormous outpouring of love and offers of assistance, I realized early on that I had to seize *responsibility* for my own healing I alone could do the work. Like fear, grief must be addressed directly. There was every temptation to avoid even thinking about the loss, to become purposely distracted by activity, and yet there was a voice in the recesses of my heart that warned me to pay full attention to what was happening around me and in my life.

This voice seemed to come from an observer who has accompanied me throughout my life. It is not the fellow who sits on my shoulders at times to criticize me and vocalize what I should have done, or one of those phantoms who fill the room to urge me to do thus with my life to conform to the wishes of the majority. No, this observer provides gentle, heartfelt guidance that is repeated just below the hum of the monkey chatter that invades our minds. And this guidance directed my attention to the significance in my life of Donna's loss—not as a warning of dire consequences if I did not pay attention, but rather as a special invitation to greater growth. The observer went on to say that no one can provide the focus that I can. And what was the promise if I took up the invitation? By seizing this opportunity, I would discover that the grief dissipates into a door opening to a treasure chamber. The voice was

---

14   Mathew 8:8

clearly showing me God's promises to take the Devil's work and turn it around to something good. I could take Donna's untimely and tragic death and turn it around to the beautiful things she represents.

I was in New York with one of my daughters when I wrote this poem. This was a time when I became acutely aware of the importance of remaining in the Now. Indeed, to the present day, four years after the loss of my spouse, remaining in the present has become a critical ingredient in healing and self-discovery.

Some Answers

What is Now?
It is not last night, or
Her anticipated departure
Next week,

It is not distracted
By future choices,
Burdened with past regrets.

This present moment
Acknowledges
The I AM deep within
Who roams supreme
In the cavern of the heart.

And this I AM?
It is a guiding and enduring light
That seeks expression.
In consciousness.

Rule 2 Exercise—How much easier would it be to turn to someone who proclaims you are healed, or to a prescription drug? Would the whole benefit of this struggle for growth and healing be lost?

Review Appendix A for a list of common emotional reactions to grief. Develop your own list from those offered, perhaps naming your own unique reactions. Go down the list and check those that apply, then repeat the exercise in a couple of weeks. Continue the practice once a month or so to see how those reactions signifying acute or chronic grief lessen, and how others demonstrate that your emotional balance is being restored. Repeat the exercise again in a year, then in two years. This exercise was of great personal value to me as it helped me to monitor my recovery, even growth.

My Thoughts

My Thoughts

My Thoughts

Rule 3—Don't rely upon the passage of time to heal—time offers only offers a snapshot of your progress or lack thereof.

> *There is only a single instant of time that keeps renewing itself over and over with infinite variety.*[15]

Prayer—Thank you for bringing this quote to me. Help me to penetrate its deeper truth.

Response—What a challenge to reduce the vast memories of the past and the illusions for a future to this single moment that I will refresh eternally for you. And though you think at first you are being told to tread water in a present, I am telling you first there is only the present, and second, the present is your invitation to experience eternity. The parting of the curtain or the veil to the other side is through the portal of the present moment. On the one hand, a great burden is lifted from you in this truth, and at the same time, you are challenged to journey to a depth unthinkable before you experienced deep loss.

Reflection—Four months after Donna's passing, I was at the school to pick up Chris. The principal met me and asked how I was doing. I responded in a positive manner. She said, "Time is a great healer." I nodded agreement, but I wanted to say that it isn't time that is healing me but the support of friends and family and the inner stirrings of my soul through God's grace. After all, what is time—the clock on the mantel piece, the watch on my wrist?

I remember reading Thomas Merton's *Seven Storey Mountain*[16] when I was seventeen years old. Merton's autobiography recounts his journey from agnosticism to entering the Trappist monastery. At the time, it was a powerful book which sold many copies and had a deep impact on my spiritual development. The book made a lasting impression on me. Ten years later as a CIA case officer I purchased a copy of the book in a small bookstore in Warsaw. I reread the book and could accurately describe who I was at seventeen, and more importantly, who I had become. I discovered that the changes in me were the outcome for someone fully engaged in life—at that time college, graduate school, applying for and being accepted by the CIA, training from agent-handling to parachute training, marriage with two children, and then the assignment to Warsaw.

My father was in deep mourning from the time my mother died in 1987 until his own death in 2003. He provided the perfect model that I choose not

---

15   Chopra, Deepak. *The Book of Secrets: Unlocking the Hidden Dimensions of Your Life.* New York: Harmony Books, 2005, 198.

16   Merton, Thomas. *The Seven Storey Mountain.* Orlando, Fla.: Harcourt Brace & Company, 1948.

to follow—someone who is waiting for time to heal, but it never does. During those years following my mother's death, he talked of life in the past tense. "I had it all," he would declare and go back to his reflections, ignoring the vibrancy of the Now in all its presence.

Residing close to the surf, I have spent many hours in reflection of life's mysteries. The ocean provided the setting for the following poem.

Beyond The Breakers

In the thunder of the wind
I hear a whisper—assurance
Rushing above the surf
As it blows tears dry.

Salt foam from whitecaps
Screeching across the flat,
Transforms puff billows
Into cotton candy.

The declining sun
Still warmth
Bristles brush-sand
Into a golden sheen.

I am graced
Out far beyond the breakers
Where serenity is not measured
In distance and time.

But exalted I explore
An ancient path
To an inner consciousness of soul
Where truth reigns.

But whoever lives by the truth comes into the light, so that it may be seen plainly that what he had done has been done through God.[17]

---

17   John 1:21

Rule 3 Exercise—After experiencing a tragedy, do you remember when your wish—even momentary—was to wake up from the nightmare and resume life as you knew it? Describe the person you were at the beginning of your season of grief and take stock—as a bystander would—of who you are becoming.

My Thoughts

My Thoughts

My Thoughts

Rule 4—Awakening in a "dark wood," as Dante writes in the opening lines of the Divine Comedy, be assured that you are not lost.

Nel mezzo ... del cammin ... de nostra vita ... I retrovai ... per un oscure selva.

In the middle of the road of my life
I awoke in a dark wood
Where the true way was wholly lost.[18]

Prayer—Help me to grasp the meaning of these words that come down to me from the past.

Response—You have yet to understand with confidence that I am there to reach you in whatever your circumstances. If you read literature, I am there providing you what you need to progress along the path. If you are a car mechanic, an engineer, a fellow stocking shelves, a homemaker, an artist, I am there as well. Your obligation is to pause and listen.

Reflection—In the time immediately after Donna's passing, I began rereading David Whyte's *The Heart Aroused*. Whyte is a Welsh poet who resides in the United States and conducts seminars for the business community, introducing concepts on how to encourage a creative environment among corporate managers. The translation above is taken from Whyte's translation of Dante's opening lines.

I could immediately identify with the words because indeed I was in middle life—even later unless I was to equal in years some of the biblical elders—and I had found myself on a life path that I did not expect and for which I was unprepared. Further, my surroundings were dark indeed without Donna.

It was not long after rediscovering this passage and identifying with its description of my situation when I learned from a colleague that a therapist used the Divine Comedy to help him heal his Viet Nam-inducted post-traumatic stress syndrome. As I reflected deeply on the passage, I learned much about myself and coping with my situation.

Most of all, I learned that I was not lost—just disoriented in the new surroundings. I came to accept that I was where I was supposed to be. I wondered where I had heard this truth before; perhaps from one of Tom Brown's books[19] outlining the initiation process in a vision quest. This same colleague counseled me to remain for a time "in the wood"—there was no rush to exit.

---

18   Whyte, David, *The Heart Aroused,* New York, Doubleday, 1994, 26.

19   For an introduction to Tom Brown's books, see *The Quest*. New York: Berkley, 1991.

And so, I became determined to take it all in—the sounds of my racing heart, the smell of fear, the void of darkness, the deep sadness of losing my mate and the tears—everything. Returning from a walk before dawn, I knelt before a set of chimes that Donna had placed in the ground before our home and I struck the chimes in a quick, methodical beat, filling the immediate area with the sounds of a new dawn.

I have since come to appreciate that indeed I was not lost, just in the process of gaining my balance in order to resume my journey. But before I did so, I also came to understand that there were many treasures for me to discover in the darkness, including acceptance, faith, compassion, resilience, commitment, strength, and patience—all of these gifts triggered by my loss—if I was willing.

Ever vigilant, some would say protective, my initial reaction to her passing was to ask myself was there anything I could do for her. "Left Behind" describes my confusion and determination. It was written soon after Donna's death.

Left Behind?

Have I been left behind,
Or am I following too close?
Hard to say in this dark wood
Where the path seems lost.

Listen for the footfall.
Catch a glimpse
Of the shadow guide
Somewhere up ahead—
Or quite alongside.

I risked being left, even lost
Had I not abandoned
All for the chase—
A captive taken unaware and
I in precious pursuit.
I sense they are just footsteps early.

Once I imagined time slowing
To accommodate eternity—
And it did, but I too often
Browsed and groused the future.
Returning Now, I Am,
Not was, nor will I be.

Perhaps, my goal is not before me
But within—where spirals meet.

Rule 4 Exercise—As a child I used to adjust to the darkness by lying still and listening. Not a bad formula for an adult! What works for you? Find a place to sit quietly in a dark room where you will not be disturbed. Spend some time quietly clearing your mind of the events of the day. When you are settled and your breathing is steady and relaxed, imagine that you are in a treasure chamber of dreams. What do you "see" awaiting your touch? Be sure to note what you observe when the lights go on.

My Thoughts

My Thoughts

My Thoughts

Rule 5—Release anger, regret, and guilt, and introduce forgiveness.

> *Forgiving is a serious business because it is basically for our own spiritual, emotional and physical benefit. We may or may not establish a new relationship with the person who injured us; that is not the heart of forgiveness. When we forgive, we finally stop hurting ourselves, hand the whole matter over to God.*[20]

Prayer—What more can you teach me about forgiveness?

Response—Forgiveness is soul and heart altering. It is during the process of forgiveness that you learn an essential ingredient of love, for without the capacity to forgive there is no love. The more you are able to forgive, the deeper are you able to love. Life is filled with paradoxes and this one is provocative in its truth as tragic loss leads to the capacity to experience great joy.

Reflection—My father came to live with us after my sister died. Hardly a day went by without his mentioning his deep anger at his father, my grandfather, for the abuse that he, his mother, and his siblings faced during my grandfather's alcoholic bouts. The anger had been vivid for my father for many, many years and he carried it as if it were a treasure to be guarded at all costs. Clearly, it had taken a toll. My father was an angry person with no friends—except my mother.

One day as I was driving him home from Starbucks, I interrupted his daily criticism of his long-departed father and said, "I know the unhappiness your father caused, but tell me something funny you experienced with him." He paused, looked at me for what seemed minutes, and then he described an experience with his father that occurred when he was eight years old.

His father had rented a horse and wagon to sell a shipment of bananas to the local inhabitants of the tenements in the South Bronx. The horse was blind and on its head it wore a straw hat. It swayed as they made their way down the street, with my father shouting, "Bananas for sale." Unfortunately, my grandfather's attempt at becoming an entrepreneur along the lines of the founders of United Fruit was not successful. Though he had lined up cheap labor, transportation, and product, the blind horse had a voracious appetite and consumed the profits.

---

20 Mennonite author Peter Dyck, as reported in *The Virginia Pilot*, October 8, 2006. Dyck's quote concluded a letter from a Mennonite following the killing of the young girls in Nickel Mines, Pennsylvania.

An amazing healing occurred in the recounting of this life experience. My father was freed from the anger he carried for so many years. He never again mentioned the hatred he once held for his father.

When Donna departed so suddenly in that tragic accident, I felt no anger at the Creator, the fellow who hit her, the hospital attendants, etc.—though I was deeply distraught. I let it go with the thought that at two hundred thousand feet the situation might make more sense to me, but at sea level I couldn't do much more than accept. I also knew from my father what anger could do to delay my healing and recovery. Again, my father proved to be the teacher or model that I needed to drive home this truth. When I learned that the man who drove into Donna died himself after three months in a hospice, I prayed for him.

Earlier, several friends in the legal profession suggested that I sue the estate of the person responsible for the accident. With no hesitation, I rejected the idea and said that I would be satisfied with what the insurance policy allowed even if it was only ten thousand dollars. Much later in court I told the presiding judge that the reason for my decision was to speed the release of the anguish the accident caused. The judge later thanked me openly for sharing my story and only wished that others could hear it and perhaps be similarly released from the suffering that they carry into and out of the courtroom.

I served in Beirut at the onset of a civil war in 1975. An experience during that time inspired this poem.

A Burst of Lead

Fingering the burst of lead,
Shark-rough after glancing the wall,
I contemplate my fate.

Too light to weight paper
This inch of bruised metal
Hurled from afar
By a stranger intent on malice.

"He is innocent," I say.

He did not know me.
He did not reach me.
He did not see me fall.

Ten years ago
Alone upon the hotel roof
He crawled its edge
And faced me.

He hugged the rifle to the ground,
Eased it slowly toward a window
Painted bright in morning sun.

I was his target.

He was so distant.
He could not hear
The crush of glass,
The hush of fear.

"He was not responsible."

Where is he today?
Sidon, Tyre, Beirut?
Damour, Damascus, Tripoli?
Paris, Athens, Bonn?

Or is he dead?

Ten years of strife
Do take their toll.
If he were fifteen then,
Could he have survived to twenty-five?

Youth, soccer, laughter
Succumb to anger, fear, and hate.
Civil war consumes the young.
Spiritless and aged they become.

He would not have heard me cry,
Nor heard from those who love me,
If sun glare had not
Confused his sight.

I am alive, well, forgiving.

Rule 5 Exercise—Where in your body do you hold sorrow and grief? How about joy and forgiveness? What would it take to expand the hold of Love throughout? Select someone who has hurt you unjustifiably and whom you have not totally forgiven, if at all, though many years might have passed. Contact that person and ask that person to forgive you for withholding your own forgiveness.

My Thoughts

My Thoughts

My Thoughts

Rule 6—Experience the support of ancestors

> *Oh, may this be the one who will bring forward*
> *The good, true and beautiful in our family lineage;*
> *Oh, may this be the one who will break the harmful*
> *family patterns.*[21]

Prayer—I more often have seen my actions as influenced by those who raised and mentored me. Less often I have seen that these same ancestors are there to support me in my trials. Help me to understand more clearly how ancestors can be there for me as those angels who have protected me over the years.

Response—Ancestors and ancient mentors and guides form a choir of supporters who offer their prayers of grace and assistance. Help and support await only your openness to their teachings which are passed on through generations.

Reflection—On the way to the church for Donna's service, I was aware of the support of my ancestors. They seemed to be lined up behind either shoulder—the Italians on the left and the Scots on the right. That support became manifest when I recall the strength, if that is the word, as I greeted calmly and gently everyone present—almost two hundred friends and family members—and did the same at the conclusion of the service and during the reception that we held at our home. What a surprise for someone who can become quite emotional at farewells—even the less permanent ones.

---

21 From an old European song, passed down through an oral tradition, stating how ancestors may support us as described in Angeles Arrien's *Four Fold Way: Walking the Paths of the Warrior, Teacher, Healer and Visionary.* San Francisco: Harper, 1993.

In honor of my older son's marriage and the ancestors, I once wrote this note to his future father-in-law.

> *Dear Art:*
>
> *John's great-great-grandfather was born on the Isle of Skye in Scotland in the late 1840s. He left the island around 1860 for Glasgow—some two hundred and fifty miles distant—in search of work. Finding nothing in the big city, he signed aboard a ship bound for New York as a coal stoker.*
>
> *On the night before the ship tied up alongside a pier on the Hudson side of Manhattan Island, he decided to remain in the U.S. The next day, he requested shore leave and withdrew only a portion of his wages. He didn't want anyone to suspect his true intentions. Once on the tar-covered gangplank, he walked casually across the border into America. Had someone shouted, "Hey, Douglas, where are you going?" he might have broken into a run and disappeared into the city. But no one called.*
>
> *He settled in the Bronx, found work stoking school furnaces. He married Kate Whelan, who had arrived earlier from Ireland to work as an upstairs maid. They raised four children.*
>
> *Among his quiet pleasures were to read the* Herald Tribune *by the window, eat vanilla ice cream, and drink a pint of beer at Jablonski's pub before his namesake and grandson—John's grandfather—summoned him for dinner at Kate's direction.*
>
> *May this bottle of Talisker[22] honor the islander who abandoned Skye for New York so that his great-great grandson, John, could fall in love with and marry your daughter, Jennifer Keegan.*

---

22 Talisker is a single malt scotch whiskey produced in the Isle of Syke's only distillery.

Rule 6 Exercise—As never before, I share a kinship with those who preceded me, as well as those who will follow, and I am determined to win their favor with my love. If you do not already have one, create a modified family tree with those relatives that have passed on. Imagine the support that each would lend to you in this situation. Remain with the emotions that arise. Identify where they would position themselves near you in this time of stress. Now experience their love and support and describe your thoughts and feelings.

My Thoughts

My Thoughts

My Thoughts

RULES 7-11

Soon after Donna's loss, I attended several sessions with Larry Crawley-Woods, a grief counselor from Hospice in Martinsburg, West Virginia. In one of our first sessions, he explained the process of grieving and helped me to track the common reactions to grief in terms of acute and chronic suffering. Immediately following the loss, one's suffering is so severe that uncontrollable sobbing, inability to sleep, and total loss of appetite are quite normal.[23] As the months passed, I discovered that the more acute signs yielded to a manageable discomfort with some actual benefits.

For example, within two to three months after the loss, signs such as guilt, hopelessness, despair, and disbelief remained, though in a milder form, while a desire to exercise, pray, be more reflective, and expand interests emerged with a new intensity.

Three years after Donna's death, I still experienced loneliness, restlessness, sadness, and occasional tears, but in the same time period my interest and curiosity increased. I had become more—perhaps permanently—reflective, valued relationships more, dispensed compassion more freely, loved more, experienced the Present more consciously, and I definitely laughed more deeply.

The following Rules emerged for me as the acute suffering of loss eased.

---

23 See Appendix A for a list of common reactions to grief. I have expanded and/or modified the list that I first received from Larry Crawley-Woods of Hospice in Martinsburg, West Virginia.

Rule 7—Be still!

> *We are drawn to some unspeakable region, to some imageless*
> *experience, where on the pivot of all time and space, our hunger*
> *and thirst for God shall at last be stilled.*[24]

Prayer—Describe for me the stillness I seek and experience.

Response—In the clatter of life I wait for your attention in the stillness of your soul. This stillness is inexhaustible and awaits you wherever you are—even alone on a crowded beach. Find me in that stillness as I whisper to you above the clamor caused by losses and departures that suddenly leave you alone and lonely. With me, if it be your will, you need not be lonely.

Reflection—Become accustomed to a deeper, richer silence that embraces you almost between footsteps. You might discover that silence at the most unexpected time—just as you complete a task or are about to undertake another, or when all about you seem to be calamitous and the rich silence reminds you that there is a deeper presence than the activity you are doing. You are not daydreaming but have entered the Eternal Now that your suffering and grief have earned for you.

Remember there is no need to fill the airwaves with forgotten syllables or your mind with symbols and images. Simply listen to your heart beating, your lungs expanding and then emptying, and then take a deeper breath—deeper, deeper, deeper. Hold it. Let it out slowly. Be conscious about it. Savor it. In that quietness assess your state using the matrix discussed in Rule 2, or some other vehicle that helps track emotional recovery.

Alone in a hooch[25] I wrote the following perspective on how stillness can bring you to a place of peacefulness.

---

24   Cordelier, John. *The Spiral Way*. Edinburgh: Neil & Company, Ltd. 1922, 140.

25   Modified shipping container in which those assigned to Kabul lived. Incidentally, roses are indigenous to Afghanistan.

The Rose

Have you ever looked at a rose?
Really gazed at it until
You and the rose were One?

Could you sense the rose
Being in you and it puzzling
Why you can't be still,

Listen to the movement,
See the soft whisper,
Touch together Divine Wonder?

What is happening to me?
That my companion,
This blood-tip rose,

Speaks soulfully
Of a ripple-free
Presence in Love?

It must be good!
When's the last time
You looked at a rose?

Rule 7 Exercise—Become conscious of these moments of intense Presence that you experience during a day. Of what? It can be of yourself, God, a rose, quietness, what is around you, a loved one. Describe what you feel and estimate how long the moment lasts.

My Thoughts

My Thoughts

My Thoughts

Rule 8—Ritual energizes the healing process

People still need rituals and sacrifices and temples and images to make the divine mystery real to themselves.[26]

Prayer—I was attracted to ritual before I knew it was ritual. Please help me to understand how ritual eases the pain I experience in loss.

Response—Ritual gives your heart pause. Instead of beating out of control and searching for a cure or relief outside in the external world, ritual restores an interior rhythm. There is an unchanging quality of ritual, like saying words of blessing at mealtime, or awakening in the morning and praising God for another day to experience his creation. Within that interior rhythm, you find your balance. This is especially important when you experience loss of any kind. Not for the purpose of restoring that loss—ritual brings you to an ever unfolding realization that there was no loss. You are joined in a special union. In that quiet before the immediate demands of your life need attention, ritual promotes a harmony in your interior life that affects the external as well. And just for a moment, it seems you catch a glimpse of something that does not dissolve. It's called Divine Mystery.

Reflection—When it came time to discard the many flowers, mostly roses, that we received in honor of Donna's passing, I came close to packing them up into black bags and bringing them to the dump. That was my plan until I heard an inner voice suggest ritual. This is what we did instead.

On the deck table nestled high above the trees, we assembled the dried flowers. In turn Chris and I tossed one flower at a time into the woods with the vigor of competitors in a javelin contest—and we accompanied each thrust with a petition that seemed to comfort us. A selection of Chris' petitions follow:

- I love you, Mom.
- Hope you like heaven.
- Help Dad.
- Peace, be with you.
- Sorry we missed the Reconciliation.[27]
- Help Dad help me with my homework.

---

26   Griffiths, Bede. *The Marriage of East and West.* Springfield, Ill.: Templegate Publishers, 1982, 128.

27   The rite of First Confession to which Chris and Donna were heading when the accident occurred.

- I hope you see God.
- I love your smile.
- Come to me in my dreams.
- Be with me.

Later we followed another ritual that a close friend suggested. Each of the grandchildren taped messages to helium-filled balloons and released them from a nearby mountaintop. Watching the balloons drift out of sight had its own special meaning for each as they sought to communicate their last thoughts to their grandmother, or Grammy, as they called her.

Three months later, we held a family ceremony for Donna in Boynton Canyon, just outside of Sedona, Arizona. Uqualla, a Native American healer whom Donna and I had met briefly years earlier, conducted the service beneath a towering red stone spire named Kachina Woman by the natives. In addition to the ten adults present, our ten grandchildren participated in the celebration.

Ritual helps to formalize the recognition of loss in a relationship. The ceremony acknowledges a letting go and, most importantly, a moving on, a new beginning. Following the ceremony in Sedona, I wrote this poem with hot air balloons soaring in the distance.

Sedona

Dry heat
Red rock
Sage burning
Her spirit rising.

Ashes—last touch
Powder spread
Under watchful
Kachina Woman.

Wide canyon
Green brush
Steep mesa
Float upward.

Ciao!
Do zaboczenia![28]
Ja Tebya Liubyu![29]
Until we meet again!

Yellow, blue, green
Balloons drift close
Then rise and turn
As flame burns bright.

And there
At dawn
She stands, white silk,
Serene in prayer.

As I seek
Not to disturb
Many lifetimes of
Wisdom and silence.

---

28   Polish for "until our next meeting."
29   Russian for "I love you."

Rule 8 Exercise—How to incorporate ritual in our lives outside or at least complementary to the rituals of institutional religions—that is the challenge. What does it take to incorporate ritual into your life?

Design your own individual ritual to honor the passing of your loved one. Whether you choose balloons or roses is not important. Make the ritual your own, something that your loved one would understand and recognize. Include in the symbols you select words that acknowledge your love and suffering.

My Thoughts

My Thoughts

My Thoughts

Rule 9—Creative pursuits bring you into contact with the unchanging Divine healing spark within.

> *The heart of creativity is an experience of the mystical union; the heart of the mystical union is an experience of creativity. Those who speak in spiritual terms routinely refer to God as the creator, but seldom see creator as the literal term for artist. I am suggesting that you take the term creator to forge a creative alliance, artist to artist with the Great Creator.*[30]

Prayer—I have used the term *the divine spark within* over the years. What is that spark and how do I access it?

Response—The divine spark within you only has significance as you measure the body covering your interior. In fact, the divine spark is what distinguishes you from others and all creation. It is that unique stamp that provides recognition of your divine origins. As bold as that might sound, you are in this world to bring to fruition, to consciousness, the divine in all your actions. It is that bringing into actuality that serves to demonstrate divine urgency in the process of creativity—not limited by the arts but inclusive of every gesture, word, and prayer.

Reflection—I have always written, professionally and for pleasure. In the latter category, I wrote an unpublished novel related to international terrorism, and a screenplay. During the Lebanese Civil War, I used to sketch scenes along the Corniche, the broad avenue that hugs the Mediterranean Sea, from my balcony in Beirut—once I was assured that another round of fighting was over and the pedestrians appeared again on the streets.

However you tap into your creative spark in times of grieving, whatever it takes, tap, tap, and then tap some more. Since Donna's passing, I have kept a journal, had a small volume of poetry published, and completed a novel on my experiences observing the Saudi royalty. I touch the Divine spark until I burn. The following is a letter I wrote to Donna days after her passing. In retrospect I see that it provided an early access into the interior where the Creative Spark reigns supreme.

---

30 Cameron, Julia. *The Artist's Way: A Spiritual Path to Higher Creativity.* New York: G.P. Putnam's Sons, 1992, 2.

I look over at your photo and I feel you are quietly watching me. I wonder—want to know—if I am doing OK. I guess I need reassurance from you as I did when you were around. Not sure you would approve of Chris sleeping in our bed—but I feel sleeping in our bed on your side reassures him and may help him to open up, to heal.

A neighbor offered to be a sounding board for me since she had experienced deep suffering after the loss of her mother. I responded to her in an e-mail message with what is going on in my heart.

I feel controlled—not allowing myself to linger on what it means that you are gone. I could sure use some sign from you that all is well.

The children bought me a bear print from Tari's Cafe[31] and I hung it in the library so I can see it easily from my desk.

Crazy thought—and I suspect there will be many—is that your departure is linked somehow to the Power of Love.

---

31   Restaurant in Berkeley Springs, West Virginia. Bear was Donna's power animal in her shamanic study.

Rule 9 Exercise—How do you experience in your life the creative process and with whom do you share the joy of creation? I once attended a workshop conducted by a noted cross-cultural anthropologist, Angeles Arrien.[32] We were required to write a haiku each day over a two-week period. Haiku is a mode of Japanese poetry. The most common form for haiku is three short lines. The first line usually contains five syllables, the second line seven syllables, and the third line contains five syllables. Haiku doesn't rhyme, but paints a mental image in the reader's mind. This is the challenge of Haiku—to put the poem's meaning and imagery in the reader's mind in seventeen syllables over just three lines of poetry! Take out a piece of paper and write a draft haiku that you will later copy in the space below. Do not hesitate to write, as the spirit moves, a haiku to reflect daily routine. Here is an example by the poet Basho, from Japanese classic literature.[33] Note that translation into English affects the syllabic order.

> *Monks' feet clomping*
> *Through icy dark,*
> *Drawing sweet water.*

What follows is an example from a friend, Vicki Jenkins.

> *The day is scheduled*
> *Still nothing stays in rhythm*
> *Order is its own.*

---

32 Angeles Arrien, PhD, is an anthropologist, author, educator, and corporate consultant. She lectures and conducts workshops worldwide, showing the bridge between cultural anthropology, psychology, and comparative religions. Her work reveals how indigenous wisdoms are relevant to our families, professional lives, and our relationship to the Earth. For an introduction see her book *The Four Fold Way: Walking the Paths of the Warrior, Teacher, Healer, and Visionary.* New York: Harper Collins Publishing, 1993.

33 Basho, 1644-1694, is considered the first great haiku artist. He changed his name from Matsuo Kinsaku.

My Thoughts

My Thoughts

My Thoughts

Rule 10—Write your own life script. Don't allow anyone, even out of love, to do it for you.

> *For years copying other people,*
> *I tried to know myself.*
> *From within, I couldn't decide*
> *What to do.*

> *Unable to see,*
> *I heard my name being called*
> *Then I walked outside.*[34]

Prayer—Sometimes I come upon a poem, a situation in life, or read an incident in the daily newspaper that I sense applies to me, something I can learn from, but the essential meaning still escapes me. Provide me the insight to catch the meaning of this quatrain as it applies to me.

Response—I encourage you to "walk outside" and take in the full dimension of these words: It is not all about you. You will find meaning in community with others as you administer to them in your grief, and, most importantly, as you accept their administering.

Reflection—Many of my decisions—to study the classics at Fordham Preparatory School; to take Russian at college; to pursue Russian Studies after my unsuccessful first year of law school at New York University; to reach for a career with the CIA instead of a more traditional corporate path; to marry for love; to accept so-called hardship assignments and focus on counter-terrorism; and so many others—invited sometimes-contrary advice from those standing in the wings and observing.

Only when I have the courage to say thank you to loved ones and still move forward with my decision am I empowered, despite the natural setbacks any path reveals during life's journey.

So many well-intentioned and loving friends and family had all sorts of ideas for me—sell the house, move closer (to what or whom?), don't date—it is not time, why don't you … (spend this weekend, do this, don't do this, and on it goes). I have been blessed with independence, health, optimism, and a curiosity to see around the next corner, and I have also been blessed by an expanding community of family and friends who bless me.

---

34   Sufi poet Jelaluddin Balkhi Rumi represents the mystical exploration of Islam. For an introduction to Rumi, see *The Essential Rumi* translated by Coleman Barks, Castle Books, 1995.

I encouraged my children as they approached those significant milestones in their lives with, "I still didn't know what I wanted to be when I grow up." I love that aspect of me, a spirit ranging in ever-widening circles while spiraling deeper in communion with my Source.

I was inspired to write "The Fisher" as I observed an elderly (must be careful whom I call elderly!) gentleman alone at a table in Starbuck's reflecting a certain Light.

The Fisher

Gray short clipped beard
He gazed through the window
Of the coffee shop, a Dallas Cowboys
Sweatshirt tucked in his pants.

His thoughts sounded words
In a language I understand,
Memory, pain, joy,
Long years do that.

Crisp, trim, balanced—
A gymnast who never relented,
A glow, some would say
An aura of blue light, wash over him,

As it would far off
From shore on a stormy sea
As he quelled inner turmoil,
Searching for the Light.

Presence, patience,
Serenity, acceptance,
This Fisher proclaims silently
To all who listen NOW.

Rule 10 Exercise—Who wants to write your life script? Has she or he selected a producer and director—and have you acquiesced? Your assignment is to develop a script for someone playing a role involving a traumatic experience of loss or rejection. Outline the events or experiences you would incorporate into this person's life: where he/she will live, work, play—and even what type of relationship the person seeks and with whom. That person is you.

My Thoughts

My Thoughts

My Thoughts

Rule 11—See the shock that precedes loss and precipitates grief and deep mourning as the other side of the surprise experienced in an unexpected expression of love. Together they reflect the harmony of the Divine countenance.

> *It did come—the day when the grief became small. For what had befallen me and seemed so hard to bear became insignificant in the light of the demands which God was now making. But how difficult it is to feel that this was also, and for that very reason, the day when the joy became great.*[35]

Prayer—Continue to expand my understanding of this paradox.

Response—You must continue to let go—let go of what you perceive you lost, let go of preconceived notions of how things should be, let go of the notion that you are in control, let go of the notion that you will live forever in this body. Let go and observe the flowing water that results when a dam is dismantled. It is in that release that you will find the balance between joy and grief, and if you really let go, you will discover at the deepest level that joy wins out.

Reflection—Clearly, the acute aspects of grief must ease before you can gain sufficient perspective to address Divine Humor. But when you are able, there are extraordinary treasures waiting for you. Your loss will not be nearly as daunting as you once considered it. You will begin to harvest a hidden value, perhaps even a secret purpose, in your loss.

For so long, I sought to find that sometimes hidden purpose in loss or setback. I have taken the search so far that I see a lighter side to a serious event, even using what can be described as black humor, where at first glance none appears. Could the fact that I was raised in the Bronx have anything to do with this approach? (I jest.) For many years, I have refused to accept the figurative wine glass inadvertently knocked over at a formal reception as anything but a good omen—somewhere in the world.

As I look out through the window in my library, I consider the truth contained in this Rule. Reflecting upon the loss that prompted such grief, in time I was able to parse the experience. With the emotional turmoil settling, I could identify the key elements of the tragedy in the first instance and later see where those elements surfaced elsewhere.

It is still difficult for me to write about the shock I experienced at the scene of the accident when I learned that Donna and Chris had been struck in a crosswalk on their way to church. I had talked with her an hour earlier via cell phone. When I arrived at the church I noticed a couple of police cars blocking

---

35   Hammarskjold, Dag. *Markings.* New York: Alfred A. Knopf, 1964, 90.

the main street in front of the church. My first reaction—however irrational—was that a church dignitary was attending the ceremony.

I remember asking the lady who worked in the rectory what was going on. She burst into tears at my question and asked me to speak to the police officer. I still did not suspect anything when a police office approached and asked if I was Mr. Douglas. He then proceeded to tell me that there had been an accident and that Christopher seemed OK but had been taken to the local hospital. I also recall seeing a man about my age, forlorn, leaning against the lamppost and staring at me. Later, I realized that he was the driver of the vehicle.

Distressed, but thinking that my son was the accident victim—and not Donna—I rushed to the hospital to see him reading to the hospital chaplain. It was only then that I realized that Donna was the focus of the hospital's efforts, and this was confirmed by the doctor's explanation of the seriousness of her condition and the need to move her to another hospital immediately. I remember vividly seeing her wheeled by me on a gurney—unconscious, but seemingly peaceful.

Hours later, in the second hospital, the excellent medical staff confirmed that her brain stem had been shattered. With one of my daughters and my son present, I agreed to have Donna taken off life support.

Later, Christopher recounted how they had been struck in the crosswalk with such force that Donna's shoes had been knocked off, and how Christopher recovered the shoes and placed them on her feet. To this day, events surrounding this tragedy continue to emerge as this young boy continues to heal.

On another plane—once I had time to take a deep breath, pause, take stock of what had just happened in my life—the shock and surprise were for me no different from the shock and surprise when confronted with any unexpected event in this life drama.

It is for each of us to pull in each experience, be it joyful or tragic, to savor it as we do a fine wine, or as we react to a description that causes us to look up from the book to take in the meaning, or to a scene that causes a skip in our routine. It is in that pause, that gap of always thinking and verbalizing, that the deeper truth is revealed. It is with that *surprise* in not anticipating the ending, in that finality, that we discover a deeper meaning to life's events, and here that we discover a capacity to grow spiritually.

We realize at those times that we are on stage or even in a dance with those we lose and release, and all we can do is to remain in the present, relishing that present, with no anxiety of trying to anticipate the ending. This sense influenced the creation of "Curtain Call."

Curtain Call

Sometimes it seems
We are on stage
To play our part
In earnest.

Perhaps, the arts attract us
To reflect and contemplate
As we are readied
For our role.

Films, theater, drama,
Music, literature, painting
Expand the linear experience
And community of our solitary lives.

Will we next participate in tragedy, comedy,
Or will a joyous celebration
Be our pull—all together?
No doubt surprise will be our fate.

The only requirement
In this Divine theater
Is that we be willing and
Learn our lines sincere,

Don our costumes, and
Listen for the cue,
Realizing all the time
That this is theater.

And how well we play
Expands our soul
And our consciousness
Of One so Divine.

Exercise 11—How can I express without guilt the enormous joy, the deep laughter, and the consuming love I now experience with those around me and with whom I come into contact? Recently, a passing acquaintance described me to someone as *that laughing man.* Grief and tragedy have served, paradoxically, to open these portals of my soul.

View *The Truman Story.* Consider the texture of Truman's life before the surprise of his environment becomes clear. Reflect on the steps he decides to take to bring authenticity into his life and the risks he faces as he assumes responsibility for his own script.

My Thoughts

My Thoughts

My Thoughts

RULES 12-16

You will discover that the Rules are not exclusively associated with grieving over the loss of a spouse or intimate partner. These rules have relevance to other life crises such as rejection—as I was soon to learn in the separation and divorce I experienced. They can apply to the loss of a job, failing health, or any setback that seems to hurl one from his or her anticipated life path. Such setbacks, like profound grief, exhibit an acute and chronic stage by which to measure their severity or enduring nature. Though the stimulant for the grief might vary, true grief occupies a unique place understood only by the select few who approach the region consciously.

Rule 12—Befriend depression. Give him a name and allow him to bring to the light those hidden, unarticulated fears lurking in the darkness. Remember, he is taking you to a place of clarity and purpose.

It is in aloneness we finally seek His face.[36]

Prayer—Guide my steps in the quiet and aloneness that sometimes gives way to depression.

Response—In the silence you find me, and your loneliness can yield to a community of souls that stretches far beyond what you believe is possible. In respecting depression, learn to accept what is unfolding in your life without judgment or any attempt to hold on to what was familiar. See in depression an energy that seeks to burst out and prepare you for the adventure on which you have embarked.

Reflection—While I have never been considered the last of the gypsy dancers, I had rarely experienced the depth of depression that I did and sometimes still do since Donna's passing. For example, this evening, as I write—after dinner with Christopher in the shower—I feel low. Why? Well, I am still mulling over a conversation I had with a friend concerning our relationship.

So what do I do now? I call upon Killian. Yes, Killian. That is the name I gave to my depression and indeed he is my friend because he identifies my hidden fears.

"OK, Killian, help me out," I said.

And Killian always responds. He said, "Terry, your greatest fear is that this relationship is ending and you don't know how to let go. You don't want to walk away. You are deeply concerned that your friend doesn't love you and you don't know what to do to change her orientation; you are not accepting that her feelings are her own and you can't control them, nor would you want to."

He continues, "You talk about being in the Now, yet you allow the past—her past—which doesn't exist anymore than your past—to haunt you. You allow fear of failure to interfere in your relationship. You permit your Soul-Self to be buffeted by an ego that seeks to reassume its position of authority. And finally, you seem to be waging this battle alone, with no one readily available in whom you could confide without appearing weak and needy."

"So what do I do?" I ask.

The reply is immediate. "Bring the fear of inadequacy into the light of your strength. Reflect upon who you are, from where you came, and where you are heading. Accept that this relationship might end, but realize that you have

---

36 A friend gave these words to me.

already demonstrated that you are able to survive a soul-shattering loss and are more compassionate, loving, and understanding than you were before. Be thankful, if the relationship does come to a close, that the emotional ties are not deep. Embrace the support of family and friends that awaits you. Accept God's will in all aspects of your life and remember that everything is on schedule, especially in love relationships. And just when you feel lowest, reach out and help someone in need."

Service serves to convert depression into a healing energy. To illustrate this fact, let me describe a visit to Aschiana, an orphanage in Kabul. My assignment there in 2005 coincided with the presentation of new athletic shoes for the six hundred children. The shoes were purchased with funds donated by CIA personnel assigned to Kabul.

In an increasingly cold, wet, rainy day the children lined up on a modest playing field in front of a portable covered stage. The girls—aged from six years to sixteen years old—stood in order on the left and the boys on the right. The shoeboxes had been carried earlier from the storage area to the stage and arranged according to size and sex. The distribution process began with the booming voice of the principal, a dark-complected man in his mid-forties who was dressed in what is called a *shawaka mis*—the *mis* being the loose pants. Referring to a roster, the principal would call a name, beginning with the boys, and follow each name with a shoe size previously provided. The children would approach the stage one at a time, and accept the box of shoes as if he or she was being awarded a diploma. After the girls had received their boxes and were returning to their places, some would open the boxes to show their friends their prize, receiving admiring glances in return.

After the ceremony, many of the children rushed off to the residence-turned-school, removing their shoes before entering, but bringing the shoeboxes inside. Others surrounded me in the rain to practice their English, telling me about their experience in painting. Any self-absorption that depression might have caused quickly evaporated.

I wrote "Loneliness" to capture my feelings when the lady I had just married decided to leave on a trip with little advance warning.

Loneliness

Loneliness is the hum
Sounding in my right ear
That keeps me from connecting
To the white-gold, blazing energy
Channeled from afar.

Loneliness is the Ego's complaint,
Even its insecurity,
As it picks flowers,
"She loves me
She loves me not."

Loneliness is an unread newspaper,
A cup of coffee long cold,
A poem stillborn,
A sadness unearned,
A separation unrealized,
A dream forgotten at dawn.

Loneliness haunts
The future and the past, and
Seeks to disturb the present.
Yet loneliness is not intrepid,
But is the first to yield
To hope, faith, love,
And inner calm.

No fool loneliness—
He accepts defeat
As words of love left on a pillow
Before departing
Prompt a smile and assurance,
And the hum becomes a melody
Of expectation and adventure.

Rule 12 Exercise—What would you have to do to befriend your depression? Give a name to your depression that connotes a certain measure of humor or lightheartedness, respect, even acknowledgment. Conduct an introductory interview with depression as it relates to an area or event in your life that gets you down. Be as specific as you can be and ready yourself for a lively dialogue.

My Thoughts

My Thoughts

My Thoughts

Rule 13—Be prepared to re-invent yourself, and have the courage to embrace this new self without losing the accumulated gold in the old.

> *The wind blows wherever it pleases. You hear its sound, but you cannot tell where it comes from or where it is going. So it is with everyone born of the Spirit.*[37]

Prayer—Lord, there are times lately when I feel the future seems so uncertain. Please give me some insight into the truth of this verse.

Response—Clear your mind from anxiety—anxiety about the future or the past. Without that anxiety you become as free as the wind. Did you ever notice that the wind never lands hard? In accepting surprise in your life and into the present moment, you are freed from all anxiety. Spirit-born is the characteristic of one who meets each day with the trust, faith, and patience of one who doesn't land hard. Experience the Spirit in the wind.

Reflection—An old friend flattered me when he wrote, "Don't re-invent yourself, we love you the way you are and respect how you are dealing with your loss with such élan." What a gracious note from a friend of over thirty-five years! That said, however, I am re-inventing myself as I ask the eternal question, "What do I want to be when I grow up?? Or more practically, should I consider a change in jobs—even a change in career or residence. The beauty of live is that change happens.

Before I left for Afghanistan, the lady I married over a year after Donna passed and I spent three days in Key Largo trying desperately to reconnect a relationship that was drifting apart. I remember walking out onto a narrow pier in reflection and "The Pier" provided the inspiration that follows.

---

37   John 3:8

The Pier

The pier heads out
Across the water
Narrow, solid,
Well-constructed and maintained

Though sea gulls,
Ospreys and pelicans
Are its most popular visitors
From dawn to dusk.

Structure—defined,
And safety mark
The purpose of this water walk
Above the deep.

And then it happens—
Dissolution plank by plank,
Piling by piling,
And me at the reach.

So life emerges from the depth
As I relinquish form, rigidity,
And performed observables,
Allowing Force Divine to have His Will.

Exercise 13—What would it take to re-invent yourself? Does a vision of the new you emerge? To succeed, I had to dispel the phantoms of "I should" from the room. In the quiet, I found bliss. Describe what is attractive in this picture of the new you and what you need to do to realize this dream.

My Thoughts

My Thoughts

My Thoughts

Rule 14—Stay in the NOW and drill down into the eternal moment.

> *The lesson which life repeats and constantly enforces is "Look under foot." You are always nearer to the divine and the true sources of your power than you think. The lure of the distant and the difficult is deceptive. The great opportunity is where you are. Do not despise your own place and hour. Every place is under the stars, every place is the center of the world.*[38]

Prayer—Thank you for constantly bringing this truth before me.

Response—To be present in prayer, in love, in relationships, in what you do, and in service is an indication that you are learning to remain in the Now for more of your time on earth—a departure from that time when you were striving for success as defined by society. This is one of the primary lessons for you to learn. To be in the Now means letting go, no longer grasping or controlling, because the latter requires the past and future to superimpose their will. Relax, even luxuriate, in the Now and see how your joy for life matures and your loss enriches a deeper awareness of who you are.

Reflection—I am thankful that for years the Eastern philosophies have caused me to think deeply about staying in the Now. I am not sure when this interest first took root. Was it during high school when I embarked on a three-day religious retreat of silence at Gonzaga Retreat House in Monroe, New York? Or when I read, for the first time, *Seven Storey Mountain*, Thomas Merton's autobiography of his conversion and decision to enter a Trappist monastery? Or was it prompted by the time I picked up a book on Zen or the Tao? One thing I did learn—God's will is clear, immediate, and obvious—and it is not obscure.

In Poland a colleague (who later achieved ambassadorial rank) and I were invited to visit a Salesian monastery that was in need of support, still showing signs of pillaging from World War II. Our wives, who accompanied us, were required because of the cloister regulations to stay in an unheated guest cottage, but Tom and I entered the monastery building with the monk who had invited us. I still remember our surprise when we entered the monk's suite, because it was comfortably furnished and had shelves filled with books lining the walls. Our surprise was not lessened when we were treated to French cognac in Czech brandy snifters as we listened comfortably to the Mormon Tabernacle Choir's

---

38   John Burroughs was born on April 3, 1837, and died on March 29, 1921. He was an American naturalist and writer who roamed the slopes of the Catskill Mountains in New York. For a collection of his wisdom and insights, see: Burroughs, John. *The Art of Seeing Things*, Syracuse University Press, 2001.

rendition of "America the Beautiful." I guess the lesson of that experience is not to take all this spiritual stuff too seriously; perhaps, even, to view situations like the latter with the humor and detachment required.

That said, I still convinced myself that I was enlightened when it came to understanding the Now of the Eastern philosophies. However, only in these past months have I come to realize how little I understood. I wrote the following poem when I was trying to achieve clarity, still puzzled by the events that overwhelmed me with loss.

Clarity

Bullet speed
Along ice-blue
Crystal corridors,
Seeking clarity.

Squeal right,
Hold tight,
Razor-sharp angles,
Closing just ahead,

Now left, swerve deep,
Hold grip, brake now,
Accelerate up
Glass smooth surface.

Turning upon turn,
Flipping, tumbling,
Head straight,
Eyes focused

Like laser light
Past and future separate and
I collide into the Now
Where clarity reigns.

Rule 14 Exercise—Have you ever "wasted" time in the Present? Was the Now seemingly interminable? Did you ever wonder at such moments what happened to the Past and Future? In a quiet place, spend some time identifying the five most troubling aspects of your life—they can be related to health, financial concerns, spiritual challenges, past wrongs, etc. Next to each one, say whether the issue resides in the past, such as guilt over some perceived wrong, or in the future, like the fear of an early death. For those issues that seem too broad, try to be more specific in the description. Once you are done with your list, take the sting from the feared event by seeing where its relationship to the Now is missing, and, more importantly, where all is in order.

My Thoughts

My Thoughts

My Thoughts

Rule 15—Cultivate Soul-response to replace Ego as it struggles desperately to restore lost balance.

> *If you want to thrive in Baltistan,*[39] *you must respect our ways ...*
> *The first time you share tea with a Balti, you are a stranger. The*
> *second time you take tea, you are an honored guest. The third*
> *time you share a cup of tea, you become family, and for our fam-*
> *ily, we are prepared to do anything, even die.*[40]

Prayer—Help me see the role of service as I seek to overcome my grief, my loss.
Response—Another paradox: in service you are served. So in your grief, to the extent that you are able, reach out to those around you who are in need. This reaching out ought to be joyful, relaxed, quiet service. You are not looking to win awards, only to enkindle that ember within until it becomes a conflagration that warms you and those around you.
Reflection—With Soul-response, I am working on gentleness—a trait that was often subdued by aggressiveness, competitiveness, and impatience. What do I mean by Soul-response? It is that pause that keeps me from responding too quickly to criticism; the deep conscious breath I take in the midst of life's rush. As described in the quote above, it is the quiet prayer for peace in the family and beyond; the confidence in knowing that I am loved; the laughter that I generate and receive; and the sparkle in the eyes of children. You see, the list is quite endless.

Soul-response is reaffirmed in service. There are dramatic examples of service, from Mother Teresa to the selfless examples of warriors acting in generosity between violent battles. Greg Mortenson provides an example for all of us. He is a mountain-climber who re-wrote his life script to become the builder of schools for the Moslem boys and girls of Central Asia.

And so I puzzle over questions of the heart. A walk along the beach often helps me to plumb their meaning, as "Of the Heart" attempts to do.

---

39 A province located in Northeastern Pakistan.
40 Mortenson, Greg and David Oliver Relin. *Three Cups Of Tea: One Man's Mission To Fight Terrorism And Build Nations One School At A Time.* New York: Viking, 2006, 150.

Of The Heart

To learn more of the Heart
Watch a wave emerge from the depth
And fold in spray upon the sand

Hear a cormorant
Follow a line offshore
Parallel to the beach.

Wonder how crickets
Recall their refrain
Before the sun rises.

Catch a couple
Stroll in hand
Through low water.

Feel sun glisten
Off a brow
Wrinkled in glare.

Be Now to the breeze
That Spirit borne
Breathes life within.

In return, sip Starbucks
From a cup
Set deep for balance.

Rule 15 Exercise—Do you value a pause before answering a question or request? At such times, where inside do you go? For me, the pause is a focused reflection that the Soul requests, where the exterior noise is silenced and I ready myself for a deeper communication or relationship. Take a break with *Three Cups of Tea.*[41]

41   Mortenson, Greg and David Oliver Relin. *Three Cups Of Tea: One Man's Mission To Fight Terrorism And Build Nations One School At A Time.* New York: Viking, 2006, 150.

My Thoughts

My Thoughts

My Thoughts

Rule 16—Pray deeply and regularly and accept the healing.

Prayer is inspired by God in the depth of our own nothingness.[42]

Prayer—What does it take to pray?

Response—First you must be conscious of your prayer, whether you are reciting prayers that you memorized as a youth or sitting in silent adoration before the sunrise. Prayer is your communications channel to the Divine. If there was one dictate to follow, it is listen more than you mouth words. The listening will reveal to you a road map for the challenges that await you each day.

Reflection—My prayer life was quite healthy prior to Donna's passing. If nothing else, it was structured—I meditated in the morning, wrote in my journal regularly, gave praise and thanks for the many blessings that I had received, and always asked for clarification or some refinement of the Divine Plan for me.

Some years ago, I wrote an essay describing prayer for a future son-in-law. In prayer, I wrote, "We beg the Supreme Being's assistance to overcome life's daily trials; sustenance to keep us and those around us healthy; wisdom to deepen our understanding of the life and death experience; solace to comfort us in our grief; happiness to relieve us in times of trial; power to overcome the adversary; forgiveness to bring healing to mind and body; and encouragement on life's journey."[43]

The lonely stretch of beach spurred me to deeper consciousness in the following poem, "In Your Company."

---

42   Merton, Thomas. *No Man Is An Island*. New York: Harcourt Brace Jovanovich, 1955, 43.

43   See Appendix B for the complete essay.

In Your Company

From where did that humpback come?
It's still July.
Aren't the waters too warm?
She's supposed to be North.

Where did she just go?
Down deep, I expect—
To before thoughts
Arise in the mind.

There she swims
In a galaxy of Light.
Make room for me
To ride You in, or out.

Doesn't matter
How I travel, or even where,
But in Your company
I seek Peace.

Rule 16 Exercise—How do you pray when your heart feels pierced and the words seem clutched in a voiceless void? Find a comfortable spot, preferably outdoors, in which you can gain easy access in the future. Put on a favorite bathrobe or some worn garment that can withstand the cold of winter and the heat of summer. Bring an all-weather chair with you. Spend twenty minutes quietly with no agenda, no problems to solve. If you become distracted, repeat a word or a phrase that is an invitation to prayer, preferably in a language that is not your own, like *mariantha*, which is Aramaic for "Come, Lord Jesus." This becomes your mantra, a phrase that occupies your mind as you listen in silence to your heart.

After you complete the session, jot some notes about the experience. Remember there are no expectations. You have just been introduced to *centering prayer*, [44] a practice that can be found in all religious disciplines.

---

44   For more on centering prayer, see Pennington, Basil. *Centering Prayer: Renewing an Ancient Christian Prayer.* New York: Doubleday Press, 1980.

My Thoughts

My Thoughts

My Thoughts

RULES 17-24

The storm has passed though; there are still lingering clouds in the sky and the landscape still looks rather gray, perhaps even bleak. However, you must admit that you have turned a corner. Whether or not you are experiencing some relief, this chapter is about life returning to your everyday existence. It's not the same life that you had prior to your loss, but be open to the possibility that you have become deeper. As a direct result, you will experience life with much more enthusiasm and interest. You might even feel that your laughter, when it erupts, is more spontaneous and genuine, as will be your tears. And when the sun does rise, it will somehow seem brighter and more magnificent. Those on the street might even say, "Who could figure that?"

Rule 17—See yourself in union with others and their journey and with the universe.

Even in laughter, the heart may ache, and joy may end in grief.[45]

Prayer—How many times have I laughed, cried, and then laughed again as I reflected on Donna—my life with her, her passing, and the joy she showed me.
Response—Consider the spiral as a path on which you travel to the point where death and loss lose their sting as joy and humor intersect your life. Now, think of the circle as the rays of the sun bursting through a cloud formation. Realize that the clouds of grief are water vapor that is dried in the sunlight. Without the clouds, your sunsets and sunrises would lack their brilliance.
Reflection—It seems that grief serves to unite us in compassion with other sojourners. For too long, perhaps, I lacked the peripheral vision to appreciate that we are all destined to experience grief. It is grief that beckons us to return our attention to the path. As an aside, I have come to appreciate that the depths experienced in grief set the solid foundation for inexpressible and inexplicable joy.

I have also arrived at a truth that might have eluded me had I not traveled extensively. All religions and cultures are greatly influenced in seeking out answers to the following questions: what am I doing here? What's my purpose? Where did I come from? Where am I going? In answering these questions, the practitioner often discovers a universal wisdom that brings one into a spiritual union that seems to elude various and competing religions.

When a Sufi friend heard about Donna's demise, he shared with me notes[46] he had taken many years previously. He had applied them effectively when he had to cope with the loss of loved ones during the Soviet invasion of Afghanistan. A member of the Naqshbani[47] Order, he described how the Sufi leader (*Murshid*) instructed his followers (*Murids*) on the six steps that foster attention, focus, and presence. How rich are the spiritual traditions of such diverse cultures that for some represent violence and *jihad*, but for others show a kinship not found in the headlines of our newspapers. Remember that each of us is on a journey

---

45   Proverbs 14:13

46   See Appendix C for a detailed copy of the notes, plus comments as to how they might apply to a grief situation.

47   This dervish school called Khajagan ("Masters") rose in Central Asia and greatly influenced the development of the Indian and Turkish empires. The order gave rise to many specialist schools, which adopted individual names. Many authorities regard this as the earliest of all the mystical "chains of transmission."

accompanied by grieving and suffering. The guidance he offered was from a mystical tradition of Islam, designed to help one maintain focus and restore balance, because the path can be treacherous.

"In Your Love and Free—I Smile" is a poem that I could only have written as I learned to walk in grief and joy.

In Your Love and Free—I Smile

Have I matured or just learned
That love returned
Is but a distraction
As I journey to You?

Once aware, I find You
All around me,
No longer confined
To a glance of attraction.

What a lesson to learn
After so many seasons!
I preferred delay but grief and
Loss prepared me gently.

Letting go—detachment
Enhances my discernment,
Improves my vision, even vigilance
As I approach the Holy Desert of Solitude.

In Your love and free—I smile.

Rule 17 Exercise—I am reminded that at the spiritual level we are all one. In our grief we sometimes consider our experience to be beyond the suffering others have endured, we are so caught up in our own personal situation. Grief—like so many other experiences—holds a place you cannot understand until you travel there. Thank God for the grief experience, as it will surface as an important turning point in your lifetime of growth. Ask in prayer that you recognize and learn the deeper meaning grief holds for you. When through tears you utter, "Lord, use me to your purpose," you are almost there.

Take a moment to reflect on an ever-widening circle of family, friends, and colleagues who have endured great suffering over the past year. Quietly pray for their healing. Then turn to the headlines that document the suffering of the strangers who also accompany us on this journey, and pray for them. To conclude the exercise, make a note below.

My Thoughts

My Thoughts

My Thoughts

Rule 18—Identify symbols of encouragement and anticipation.

A grain of merit is better than tons of everything else, but a grain of luck is better than tons of merit.[48]

Prayer—Help me to see your love in each moment of my life through the signs with which you sprinkle my path.

Response—Those signs are everywhere—from the obvious ones represented in a phone call, e-mail, or a note from a friend that reminds you that you are loved; a lucky penny at your foot as you exit a car; or a melody with special meaning that you hear on the radio. To be loved is to be blessed. To be conscious of that love is to be twice blessed, and to be thrice blessed, share that love.

Reflection—For years, the Jaguar luxury automobile has represented a sign of good fortune for me. When I see a Jaguar, I am tempted to wave to the driver for the good tidings the vehicle conveys. Through this sign, I am reminded that life is a journey—maybe that is why a mode of transportation attracts me—and that awaiting me around the next turn there is something worth experiencing, something worth mustering that sense of youthful anticipation. The fact that Jaguars are not commonplace also heightens my delight when one crosses my path.

To this day, rain represents an auspicious sign for me. That stems from my days of rowing crew, because when it rained—not with the gusty winds—I was assured that the water would be calm. I smile upon rereading this because for Donna, rain represented depression. She grew up in Bremerton, Washington, where it always rained. A popular observation was that people from there did not tan but rather rusted.

Life is not programmed, but is an experience of unfolding surprises—neither good nor bad, just surprises. The eagerness with which we seek out the surprises adds to our conscious participation in the treasure hunt. Symbols facilitate that hunt. Perhaps they are God's way of confirming our divinely scheduled life path.

My poem "Parasail" is just that surprise, as I discover the Divine in such strange places.

---

48   In a discussion with a Sufi acquaintance in Kabul, he repeated from memory the words of Sufi mystic Sheikh Saadi of Shraz, 1184-1291, who is known for The Bostan (The Orchard) from which the quote is derived, and The Golestan (the Rose Garden). Both of these works can be viewed on www.iranchamber.com/literature/saadi/books

Parasail

What if God decided to revisit
One bright and windy day?

And suppose He chose to ride
An open-air propeller craft
Attached to a blossoming rainbow sail
And putter forty feet above the surf?

Would you not look up and wave a greeting—
Thumbs up to acknowledge His bravado?

And what about the smile returned to you?
Did He penetrate your heart, catch your longing?
Did the words He mouthed above the rush
Reveal a mysterious swirl of color, wind, and music?

It wasn't long before the engine-putter faded into ear-static,
The sail … into sun-white light.

But the vision of God-visit captured within
Restored, refreshed, a solitary visitor to an empty beach.

Rule 18 Exercise—What does it take for me to spot and interpret the signals all around me that reflect the Creator's love? I recall the time I was feeling especially sad and passed a bright yellow wooden sign—glowing like a morning sun—with the name Albright on it. I immediately read "All Bright," and got the message, "You're OK." Do you find similar encouragement around you? Remember—there are no coincidences.

Over the next week, heighten your awareness and make a note of every encouraging sign that you receive. They can be messages such as my "All Bright" experience, random acts of kindness you receive, or unexpected e-mail messages or phone calls you receive. Consider the possibility that there is a conspiracy afoot to right the balance, to heal the grief, to bring you into the Light. At the end of the week review the list and interpret the significance of the signs. Plan to incorporate those indicators into the new life that you are fashioning.

My Thoughts

My Thoughts

My Thoughts

Rule 19—Practice patient endurance.

> *Love is patient, love is kind. It is not jealous, is not pompous, it is not inflated, is not rude, does not seek its own interests, is not quick-tempered, does not brood over injury, does not rejoice over wrongdoing but rejoices with the truth. It bears all things, believes all things, hopes all things, endures all things. Love never fails.*[49]

Prayer—I have a tendency to read too quickly over words for which I think the meaning is clear. What can you tell me about this scripture reading that I might miss?

Response—It is not that you miss the meaning, but sometimes you do not apply the words to your life in relationship. These words are not meant as an indictment, but as guidance for each relationship, new or sustained, and the meaning reaches across to the full experience of love in relationship with a special person, a child, a grandchild, a friend, a passing acquaintance, a colleague. These words form a code of behavior motivated by love and consideration for and interest in that Other.

Reflection—When I was a student at P.S. 86 in the Bronx, New York, my elementary report card regularly signaled that I could do better. As I grew older, the words *could do better* were replaced in my life with *could show more patience*. And if there is any lesson for me to learn in life it is that—be more patient. I learned—or maybe heard—for the first time not long ago that one of the nine gifts of the Holy Spirit is patient endurance.[50]

I have prayed mightily for this gift—to be free from the entanglements of a future that does not exist and a past that is less substantial than the smoke from a dying campfire in the desert. Patient endurance fills me with peace and hope.

The inspiration for my poem "I Corinthians 13:4-8" came to me during a one-week visit to Beirut, almost a year before my family and I were assigned there. It was prior to the outbreak of a full-fledged civil war, when the fashion shops on Hamra Street were filled with Paris originals. There was a color and a vibrancy in the bustle of people walking along the Corniche that ringed the Mediterranean. The hotels burst with the glamour and exuberance of what was once referred to as the *jet set* and the pilots and stewardesses that made it possible. The banks held the fortunes of those who sought comfort in Beirut's stability, which was soon to shatter.

---

49   I Corinthians 13:4-8

50   See Galatians 5:22-23, "But the fruits of the Spirit are love, joy, peace, patience, gentleness, goodness, faith, meekness, self-control."

At that time, I was at the top of my game, as I would describe it. Recently promoted, soon to be reassigned from New Delhi to Beirut to assume a most responsible position, and yet ... I was reflecting deeply on a healing process that was urgent and under way in my relationship with Donna. And it was a time to allow an unfolding in grace to occur.

I Corinthians 13:4-8

Alone in the Palm Hotel
Before violence and destruction
Engulfed the Lebanon
Reading these words—
Tears flowed

Not for the malice
In the harsh glances
Hurried footsteps of strangers.

No—tears flowed
For past hurts,
Insensitive was I
To the presence of the Other.

In the years to follow
I plunged not unerringly
Into Love's power
Manifest in patience,
Trust, and forgiveness.

Now, many years later
When tears flow
They are of thankfulness
For that moment of reflection
Amidst the clamor for war.

Rule 19 Exercise—What about you? What contributes to your patience? And how about endurance? Identify an outcome of your present circumstances for which you hope or pray. Perhaps you have even set a timetable for the solution to take place. For now, release yourself from the outcome. Write below that release and acceptance. Sign and date the release. Put your pen down. Stay quiet, still, and listen to your heart and feel the peace and calm that enfolds you in that moment. After a time, jot down what you experienced.

My Thoughts

My Thoughts

My Thoughts

Rule 20—Share your journey—you are going home.

> *Do not let your hearts be troubled. Trust in God, trust also in me.*
> *In my Father's house are many rooms; if it were not so, I would*
> *have told you. I am going there to prepare a place for you. And if*
> *I go and prepare a place for you, I will come back and take you to*
> *be with me that you also may be where I am. You know the way*
> *to the place where I am going.*[51]

Prayer—Lord, sometimes I wonder if I know the way to the place where you are going.

Response—This reading is often brushed over because it seems so simple. There is this mansion sitting on a hill and if you act properly, I will reserve a room for you there. However, it is difficult for you to admit that you really do know the way to the place where you and I are going. Emphasize going and do not try to create mental images of the place on the hill. It is in the going that you find me, just as when we walked together towards Emmaus. It is in the journeying that you dance in faith and love. The journey signifies the action in faith. During the journey is when you demonstrate courage and patience because you have no idea of the length of the journey. In fact, once you accept this journey fully, you will realize that the journey never ends. To be static is to perish. Therefore, sing praise that you are making your way to me.

Reflection—Days after Donna passed I received a CD in the mail—Celtic tenors[52] singing "Caledonia" and a five-page excerpt from Hank Wesselman's book *Medicine Maker—Mystic Encounters on the Shaman's Path.*[53] in which a griffin—the mythological beast who is the protector of precious objects—comes to snatch a wandering soul to the Light. The package also contained a coaster for Griffin Brown Lager that had been placed on the sender's table in a Canadian pub just after he came upon the passage in *Medicine Maker*.

About the sender—I never met him and did not recognize his name. I wrote an e-mail message thanking him for his generosity and asking who he was. Before slipping off to sleep, I asked to see him and a picture came to me. I then remembered that months previously at a gathering he read a warrior poem. We had not been introduced. I did not know his name. The next morning I wrote another e-mail message and in the introduction I mentioned I was at a gather-

---

51 John 14: 1

52 See http://www.celtic-tenors.com/new/for a sample of the recording *Caledonia*

53 To my surprise, I discovered the book in our library. The copy was underlined by Donna, who was a serious student of shamanism.

ing months earlier where a chap had read a poem. I did not ask if he was the author, but in his reply he said, "I'm the guy."

Without question, the CD rendition of *Caledonia* did more to help me process my grief through music than all the words of comfort received. The final line of this ballad is, "I'm going home." And in time, I gained a sense that it is God Himself who is near to the brokenhearted, and from this understanding, the poem "Divine Plan" emerged.

Divine Plan

What is the Divine Plan for me?
I ask in the silence hours before dawn.

At this Moment, it is to be fully present to—
The rain striking the windows rhythmically,
The pattern of the wind off the sea,
The distant thunder and flashes of lightning.

The aroma of coffee brewing mixes with
A current that pulses through me and
Radiates presence and calm
As tears of recognition form.

Who needs to understand a Divine Plan
When His Presence is palpable?

Rule 20 Exercise—I found myself at the same table with a friend and a lady who lost her spouse of thirty-nine years—the length of my first marriage. We shared our journeys before resuming our separate paths.

Listen to rendition of "Caledonia." Write down the feelings that it stirs in you, especially as they relate to your journey. Write about your loneliness as well as about the companions who have moved up alongside you. Have you considered the benefits of a support group?

My Thoughts

My Thoughts

My Thoughts

Rule 21—Don't be surprised if you feel intensely the presence of your soul mate who has passed on through music.

> *Inspiration is a higher form of intuition, for it comes as an idea, as a complete theme with its improvisation, as a phrase creative of a poem. Inspiration is a stream, a stream of wonder and bewilderment. The really inspired person, whether a writer, a poet, a composer, or whatever may be his work, when once he has received an inspiration, has found satisfaction—not with himself, but with what has come to him. It gives his soul such a relief, for the soul was drawing from something and that object from which it was drawing has yielded to the soul, has given it what it was asking for. Therefore, inspiration may be called the soul's reward.*[54]

Prayer—I came late to an appreciation of music. Can you give more insight into the healing quality of music?

Response—At times you think communication only occurs through the words you read or utter or hear. As you know, a deeper level of communication occurs through a glance into the eyes of the beloved, the *yes* of a child, or simply through eye contact with a friend. Well, music is that kind of connection, one that doesn't need words; in fact, words distract. Listening to music, there is a spirit-reaching-out quality to the exchange that needs no words of endorsement. Another element of music makes such communication special. There is timeless-spaceless dimension to it, thus allowing your soul to range quite freely in communion with those so special to you and you to them, and even you to you. And that is where the healing occurs, again, and joy is reborn.

Reflection—Music has become so special for me in the healing process. One morning I was listening to Bach's "Concerto in A Minor for Violin, S. 1041, Andante," performed by the Orchestra of St. Luke's. I received an inspiration that Donna was there with me through music. The section was so moving that I could feel our two spirits swirling together. I felt no sorrow, but tears of joy flowed as I sensed with certainty that music was a means to feel her presence once again. More recently, I was overcome when I listened to a selection of Vangelis' score for the film *1492* that I later learned was entitled "Eternity."

Years ago, Donna and the children were evacuated from Beirut in the midst of the Civil War. I remained there, assigned to the U.S. Embassy. Each evening I wrote a letter to her and each morning I walked to the evacuation point where

---

54   Khan, Hazrat Inayat. *The Music of Life.* New Lebanon, NY: Omega Publications, 1983, 299. Hazrat is best known as an inspired musician.

I requested that my letter be deposited for delivery to the U.S. Embassy in Athens.

For three months I sent a letter each day, receiving none from Donna in return. (No one was returning to Beirut at that time.) Despite not hearing from Donna, I knew that we were communicating on another plane, maybe even at a deeper level than when we placed our heads on the same pillow each evening.

I suggest that recovering from a wrenching loss can be facilitated when you come to realize that communication with your loved one has not been lost—only altered.

An old friend came to visit me in Charles Town. We went to dinner and shared deeply of our lives and my sense of the loss I experienced. He asked me without hesitation how I communicated with Donna now.

I took some poetic license in the following poem in giving the impression that my answer to his surprising question was immediate. Rather, I only found the words to answer "How Do You Communicate" after reflecting upon the question long after the dinner.

How Do You Communicate?

"How do you communicate with her now?"
He asked—not "if."
I hesitated, thought, and answered

In the wind that sounds in my ears,
      —the chimes that ring,
      —the music not shared earlier
      —on which melodies she now rides.

In messages that tap my fingers
To form letters or touch keys.
      —insights that explain love
      —unchanging, expanding, and eternal.
      —dreams that calm soul turbulence
      —tears that resonate truth.

In the robust figure on the beach,
      —the reminder of a favorite dress
      —that one so young now wears,
      —a quiet sunset alone on the shore, or
      —an equally compelling sunrise.

In visions of golden light
      Encircling me when most vulnerable.
      —the eye-sparkle of a child, friend, and
            even lover.

Aye—how do I communicate?
Absent mind-chatter
In the silence of my soul.

Rule 21 Exercise—How do you feel a presence? This evening, if you can arrange it, set aside some time to listen quietly to a musical selection with which you are unfamiliar. Begin with Bach or perhaps Vangelis' score. The purpose is not to dwell on a shared experience with your loved one, but to uncover a fresh method of healing while savoring a joyful thought in music not tied to a past that no longer exists.

My Thoughts

My Thoughts

My Thoughts

Rule 22—Accept Your Mortality

> *Like the Tao we have no desires for ourselves,*
> *Yet all our desires are fulfilled.*
> *We have no more need for accomplishment*
> *Yet we accomplish everything.*
> *We accept the fact of death*
> *Yet find we are always alive.*[55]

Prayer—There are times when I reflect upon my future death as an observer would reflect on someone else's fate. Thank you for drawing these words to me for consideration.

Response—Death is anticlimactic for those who accept it as a transition to eternity. Allow your accumulating years to reinforce your serenity, calm, confidence, patience, detachment, and love. In so doing, you accept your mortality as the often described vehicle, or chariot, on which you thunder. With that awareness, no mythological hero rode a more determined path.

Reflection—My previously mentioned Sufi friend reminded me that in his spiritual tradition he is encouraged to visit a cemetery on a regular basis. For him, it was especially important during his years combating the Soviets in Afghanistan, because it reminded him of the passing that awaits us all.

During a short stop over in Tashkent, Uzbekistan, on my way to Kabul, on an impulse, I ventured from a broad avenue into the entrance to a Moslem cemetery with a crescent moon on the sign outside. I was interested that the gravestones were adorned with images of the deceased taken from photos of happier times. From the span of their lives carved into the stone, one could easily speculate that the deceased had been young military men. Perhaps they had fallen in Afghanistan or in Chechnya to the *mujahadeen,* or in Uzbekistan fighting for the government against the insurgents that are intent on creating an Islamic state.

While I was sitting on a wooden bench in the cemetery, jotting notes in my journal, a man of about forty years old came into view thirty feet across some gravestones. He had a dusky complexion. I did not look directly at him, allowing him the privacy he sought. He moved a bench aside so that he could kneel and prostrate himself in prayer before a particular headstone. I could hear his voice softly intone a prayer, most likely verses from the Koran. When he finished I raised my eyes and saw him wipe tears from his cheeks. As he passed me

---

55   Martin, William. *The Sage's Tao Te Ching—Ancient Advice for the Second Half of Life.* New York: Marlowe & Company, 2000, 11.

he put his hand across his heart in greeting to me—"*Salaam Aleikum*" (God is Great). I returned the salutation. It is no surprise to me that grief—the great equalizer—united us.

During this time of grieving, I have explored my own mortality, especially as it relates to relationships with those whom the odds favor will survive me. I have considered what to do now, in the Now, to limit regret at the moment of my passing. I continually seek answers to where I could "be more"—not necessarily "do more"—to promote the Power of Love not just in my immediate environs but through prayer for the entire troubled planet.

Staying engaged in the game of life, I avoid tossing my cards in early only to follow the outcome to determine if I would have won. When I was assigned to the U.S. Embassy in Poland, I used to play poker with a friend from Georgia. When a player folded his hand early, and then proclaim at the end, "If I had remained in the game, I would have won!" My friend would proclaim to those who sought victory—however illusory—without risk, "If a frog had wings, it would fly!"

And do not despair. Another close friend who was to die of cancer six months later asked me one day in a sad moment, "Terry, how many Christmases do any of us have left to celebrate?"

Without a pause I responded rather irreverently, "That isn't the question, but rather, 'How many lattes will we share together?'" And we shared one each day thereafter until the day he passed on.

Oh, I have so much to learn from what often is so elusive for me, that is, "Patience."

"Be Patient"

I fed the gulls and sandpipers this afternoon
My hoard of salty peanuts from the shell.
And here I thought the quiet beach
Would not notice my greed

So well behaved—
Taking turns, each bird and breed
Appeared at my bare feet
As before a desert prince in fealty.

And then they were gone.
Only shell trappings remained,
That is, except for one yellowed-eyed gull,
Who lingered close, peering through my eyes.

"Be patient! And they will give you wine," she whispered,
Then she too was off and I was left alone to wonder
Her genetic code or spirit that captured and repeated
Hafiz's[56] admonition to me without more peanuts.

---

56 Shams-ud—din Muhammad Hafiz (1320-1389) was a noted Sufi mystic and poet who wrote of wine as the symbol of truth, love, or the grace of God which is the heart's goal. See Paul Smith's website for more on Hafiz at www. hafizofshiraz.com.

Rule 22 Exercise—How comfortable are you with your mortality? Or, is the question, how uncomfortable are you with your mortality? Visit a cemetery at your first opportunity. Walk along in silence in a meditative state, asking quietly, "Where did I come from?" "Why am I here?" "Where am I going?" The dialogue you discover on this walk might encourage you to take a seat like I did in Tashkent. Jot down the highlights of that internal dialogue in your journal. Maybe you'll discover your purpose is as simple as helping others.

My Thoughts

My Thoughts

My Thoughts

Rule 23—Practice detachment from a desired outcome. Allow an unfolding to occur in the fullness of the present.

> *It is good that a person has a peaceful life; it is better that a person bear a troublesome life with patience. But best of all is that a person can have peace even in the very midst of trouble.*[57]

Prayer—Please give me guidance as to how to achieve this peace.

Response—It begins with a breath. Not only does a breath, a deep breath, begin the process of acclaiming peace in the midst of adversity, a breath also signifies a step along the path, followed by a second and a third. Conscious of the breath, you will find that you are pulled into the present moment that allows no disturbance to thwart the calm. You see in this moment, the moment you are in right Now, all is in harmony. Meister Eckhart proclaims your formula for achieving the peace, not some medicine-induced non-reality, but a conscious state in which you yield to a divine process as it unfolds.

Reflection—Grief is a great teacher for detachment. Just as we must learn to let go of children once raised, possessions as we seek equilibrium, or an outcome that we cannot control, so grief teaches us to let go of our loved ones as they pass from this physical dimension. The following is a letter of encouragement that I wrote to a son on this theme.

---

57   Eckhart, Meister. *Creation Spirituality*. New York: Doubleday; NY, 1980.

Dear John:

I am sorry that we were not closer last night when you called. I would have liked to explain to you in person some of the thoughts that I have—and am still developing—about trying and succeeding.

When I was your age, I thought that the harder I tried, the more success I would experience. As I got older, my experience taught me that effort did not necessarily mean success, and more importantly, my definition of success changed and continues to change. I also became aware that the success—which I strove for, prayed for, and considered my just reward—may be irrelevant and perhaps not in my best interests. I became a student of detachment. I say student because I must live many more years to understand fully the concept.

What is detachment? We are the archers, the batters, the fielders, the husbands, the fathers, the workers, the warriors, the helpers, the pray-ers, the writers, the wonderers, the creators, the seekers, who hone our skills, sensibilities, awareness, commitments, dedications as we fully engage in life's mysteries with praise, integrity, and love.

Controlling the Ego—the Me and its desire for measurable results—we immerse ourselves in life as the journey it is—and not as some destination, some terminus. With detachment, we live in the present and do not mortgage the present for a future that does not and in fact will never exist.

With detachment, we refuse to be defined by size, annual salaries, job descriptions, bank accounts, batting averages, because, indeed, we are infinitely more—a truth to be uncovered in the depths of our souls—a truth sometimes easier to express in gestures, embraces, laughter, and even tears, than in words.

So what is detachment? It's being in a racing shell, prepared for the great race of life—the starter's gun has already sounded and I am off. My only responsibility is to reach out as far as I can with balance, dip the oar into the water so that just the blade is covered, pull through strongly and evenly—one stroke at a time, using the strength and conditioning of months and months of practice.

As I focus on the single stroke, the follow-through, and the quick return, shooting my hands straight out in front of me, I ready myself for the next stroke. I am not in isolation but a participant in a larger cosmos. I hear the beat—the cadence—sounded on the gunwales with the wooden chucks by the coxswain; I feel the chill spray of the water; I taste the salt-sweat dripping down my face; I squint in the sun bright over the head of my companion before me; I hear the metal oarlocks flip back and forth rhythmically with each stroke; I sense the rush of movement from a shell on the right and another on the left.

Yet all I am charged to do—in fact, all I can do—is to reach within me mindlessly to perform each stroke as if it were the first and last because each is the same. I pray that the race go on for eternity. This prayer is answered. I cannot control the outcome. I am detached.

Rule 23 Exercise—As I sit at my desk before dawn, I am indeed humbled to have uttered years ago these words of encouragement to a son and feel the truth in tears that flow over me with the reassurance that the grieving process—perhaps above all others—requires detachment. On what is detachment based? It is based on faith and hope and joyful resignation and, perhaps most of all, on the recognition that I love.

What can we do to improve our approach to detachment? If you are a morning person, this exercise will be easy—for everyone else, my apologies. Wake one morning before dawn—even before the gray dawn. Go outside in your garden, out on the rooftop, or on a balcony, or anywhere you won't be harmed or considered a vagrant.

Allow your eyes to become accustomed to the dark and sit quietly allowing the darkness to reveal itself to you. The lesson, of course, detaches you to see the unfolding of another day. Now record in your journal what detachment and unfolding means to you at this point in your life.

My Thoughts

My Thoughts

My Thoughts

Rule 24—Reflect upon the meaning of insights that resonate in the deepest recesses of the heart.

> *I tell you the truth. Some who are standing here will not taste death before they see the Kingdom of God.*[58]

Prayer—Please bring clarity to me as I look at these words from an historical viewpoint and almost shout that Luke's audience and those following him did taste death.

Response—Do your best to put aside linear time and understand that the death of the physical body occurs in the present. So you will not taste death before you see the Kingdom. Without linear time dimension, those words are quite accurate in describing a mystery. As you understand, *the taste of death* is the significant phrase. As an ice-cream cone, you will lick it, as a last piece of apple pie you will snack on it, as a sip of hot chocolate you will taste it. You must now understand that my message is meant for all—those who have already passed from their physical dimension and those to come. It is not the time sequence that is for you to ponder, but rather the method by which you will receive a hint of what awaits you.

Reflection—Two weeks before Donna passed, we both attended a session hosted by Bob Judge, the semi-retired Jesuit who presided over St. Bernadette, the mission church in Hedgesville, West Virginia. Bob was offering a series on the Ignatian Rules of Spirituality in the Stone House that adjoined the chapel. Donna chose to attend these sessions, held after dinner, and her decision surprised me since she had traveled, I thought, far beyond what I considered a more traditional form of prayer and meditation.

At one of the sessions, Bob instructed the ten of us present in *lectio divina*—a process whereby one reads a selection of scripture, pausing on the first words that catch one's attention and remaining there in prayerful reflection. I had not read ten words of the passage when the words "taste of death" caught my attention and I remained there.

Taste of death. Taste of death. And, I thought for the first time, isn't it strange that the word taste is used? Taste is so impermanent. It passes so quickly like a taste of apple pie or even a bite of bitter lemon. Each is filed away in my memory, but is not permanently before me. Because I had lost my father just a month earlier, when he passed on in my arms as I was feeding him, I associated the insight about the impermanence of death with my father—not realizing that the true application would occur days later with Donna's passing.

---

58 Luke 9:27

And so for me, buried in that one word "taste" was a confirmation of a truth that I had come to believe—but never really tested—so many years ago, namely, that the death we experience is a temporary absence, a temporary experience. What a great reassurance to me it proved later when I would no longer hear her infectious laugh or her slippers scraping across the tiles early in the morning, embrace her, see her smile, sense her breathe next to me in bed, or be infused with her optimism, care, and love.

I wrote "Distant Star" to honor the passing of my son-in-law's mother.

A Distant Star

Beneath this bone and marrow
We are temple houses for the Divine,
Light Energies of Love
That dissolve and recreate.

Not unlike a blinking star
We pulse in—out, in—out,
A signal from afar, or so it seems,
Creating Light, dissolving, and recreating.

Our hearts do take note
As all around us we sense a chorus of acclaim
Dissolve, create, dissolve, create.
Even our breath takes note.

Though the exhale seems so deep and long,
Empties us to our Being-core, and
All we are evacuates in tears and loneliness,
Until ...

Miraculously—indeed it is a Grace—
We draw a breath much fuller than before.
And in the process acclaim and recreate,
Bless those who have gone before
To distant stars that give us hope.

Rule 24 Exercise—What meaning does taste hold for you? Go to your freezer and take a spoonful of ice cream, or perhaps a forkful of a pie you did not consume earlier. How long before the sweet taste fades? Do the same with something bitter like a lemon. Now return to the scripture passage and reflect quietly on those words, especially as to their meaning as you work through your grief. Write down your thoughts. Taste, feel, experience, absorb the sting.

My Thoughts

My Thoughts

My Thoughts

RULES 25-28

There is no denying it—you are recovering. Perhaps more slowly than you would wish, but an easing of the stress of loss is occurring, if you will allow it. What marks this stage? Your curiosity and interest in life are returning, and with this recovery you are drawing interest from others who no longer have to shoulder the full weight of your grief. Those others include family and friends, and do not be surprised if new acquaintances are attracted to the new you that is unfolding. To the extent possible, do not bring into this most important phase of your life past illusions of how you were and therefore must remain. Simply stated, be open to change with grace—and don't be surprised if, as the new self emerges, certain friends will no longer be there as new friendships are formed.

Rule 25—Don't judge, but be accepting of the twists and turns in life.

Do not judge so that you will not be judged.[59]

Prayer—Bring me to a deeper understanding of these ten words.

Response—As difficult as it is for you to comprehend, all of you are responsible for the path you have chosen. Sometimes in your fatigue, you observe the activity of someone alongside or afar and judge his or her actions measured against your own. Sometimes, you are motivated by your weariness and chose to compare whatever you observe on the surface without delving deeper into the underlying motivation. Deep down you realize the struggle of your neighbor but do little to ease the burden, rather disparaging it. Cease devoting so much energy to the choices of others. Focus instead on your own path, reserving whatever energy remains to understanding your neighbor with an open and clear mind, and praying for his or her peace.

Reflection—To the extent possible, be open to what unfolds in your life, as well as in the lives of others around you. Never say "never"—like you, I believed I could never love again. And, to the extent possible, do your best not to judge others who have embarked on a different—not better or worse, just different— path, perhaps with a different timing or different experiences and opportunities and different from what you thought should or would happen. Never say never—never!

I am astounded at the surprises that awaited and await me in my personal life. It seems that in becoming less judgmental, many more surprises await me. I could not imagine that it would be possible to experience love after my spouse passed on—but I have. And as difficult as it was for me to acknowledge my feelings, months passed before I could share these feelings with another. Once we let go of the labels so easily assigned to keep us in conformity with a model of behavior, we begin to exhibit an understanding and compassion that proves infectious in dealing with others.

Also, do not be surprised if you receive unsolicited judgment from others—friends and family alike. One of my daughters mentioned to me that in marrying again after Donna's death, I disrespected her mother. My response was simply that her mother would understand. I explained that, possibly, my regard for marriage was a compliment to Donna—though in my innocence in this new arena, it turned out to be a misjudgment. This conversation served as a call to prayer as in "Rusty Hinges."

---

59 Mathew 7:1

Rusty Hinges

A distant chapel bell
Calls to prayer.

The wind sounds
Wood chimes among the trees.

A caravan crosses in tone
The mountain pass.

And, yes, Christ was once raised high
In bell-tinged reverence.

With crystal flutes
We bless our love
And toss soul-self mix
Beyond the universe of stars
To where the planets
Turn on rusty hinges.

And we recall—or soon to be—
A love as now, expanding, discerning,
And every bit revealing
Of our origin and destination
As love warms
The tip-toes of our expectation.

Rule 25 Exercise—As I've aged, I have less over which to be judgmental—if I ever did. Life's lessons have taught me to be accepting, especially of my own frailties. I hesitate now to judge your decisions. Do you do the same? Take an evening off and view the film *City of Angels*. Think about that special person for whom you grieve and try to penetrate the truth of new understanding that you now reflect as it relates to you who were left behind.

My Thoughts

My Thoughts

My Thoughts

Rule 26—Live on the edge in anticipation of surprise—without anxiousness.

> *So the tribesmen lived only for the present, because the present was full of surprises, and they had to be aware of many things: Where was the enemy's sword? Where was his horse? What kind of blow should one deliver next in order to remain alive?*[60]

Prayer—Show me how to be more aware and receptive of the surprises that await me.

Response—Realize if you can the surprises, the answers to your prayers, are just around the corner of the present. Honing anticipation actually compels the future to become your present. With this thirst for surprise, you will find that you become an antenna for change. Consider the focus of the horseman in the reading above. You are that horseman.

Reflection—There are days that I remind myself upon waking to be on the lookout for the surprises that await me. I can still remember, years later, the spontaneous smile of a blond, chunky road construction gal as I waited to merge lanes. At the time I was wondering why life seemed to be so arduous, and her smile made a difference. Another time, I remember the surprise of receiving a call from a friend from the past who tracked me to a new location though I had not made a similar effort to discover him.

Had I planned this day, I would not have anticipated the deep insights I received in reading as if for the first time the line of John's gospel that begins this book, or expected the pleasure of wrestling with my eleven-year old son before noon, or sitting at my desk as sheets of rain pounded against the window on the canal, hearing the thunder of Alberto's winds as the first hurricane of the season passed Virginia Beach heading north.

There are times when we come so close to achieving a peak experience, only to just miss. Instead of delighting in the excitement of the chase, we fall back on what has been or could not possibly turn out. Over the years, prompted perhaps by a now forgotten dream or a passage from scripture or some inspired writer, I cultivate expectant curiosity in tracking a figure—like the one with whom Abram wrestled—that has just disappeared around the corner of my life.

And what better way to discover God but in the company of a child as in my poem "Searching Sand Crabs in the Dark."

---

60   Coelho, Paulo. *The Alchemist.* San Francisco: Harpers, 1993, 101.

Searching Sand Crabs in the Dark

We leaned against the northeaster
As we walked up the beach,
Phosphorous foam lit our way
On this moonless night.

Chris was searching tokens
From the sea for a school project,
Shells, gull feathers,
Netting—our trove.

His yellow breaker and hood
Zipped tight as he leaned back
With arms outstretched
Against the howl.

Like a sunrise
That must be shared
He instructed me
In the ways of trust.

I too tipped back,
Arms out flung, eyes closed,
As the rush
Caught me in her grasp.

Then, I think, to test my faith
She paused, I fell
Onto the smooth sand,
Felt its coolness.

Perhaps, she was only reminding me
That I grew too tall and secure.
On the beach I was a child again
Searching sand crabs in the dark.

Rule 26 Exercise—When I lived in West Virginia, I anticipated each morning the sun rising fire-red over the mountains on my drive to work. I was stunned daily by its beauty. And so, I am expectant of another day's blessing—only here with the sun rising over the expansive Atlantic Ocean. What can you do to stir anticipation and surprise in your life, or at least to increase your capability to detect the surprises that await you each day? Make a list beginning with the moment you stir in your bed.

My Thoughts

My Thoughts

My Thoughts

Rule 27—Allow inspiration to enter your life.

All true artists, whether they know it or not, create from a place of no-mind, from inner stillness.[61]

Prayer—Help me to become a true artist of healing and in comforting others as I have been comforted.

Response—You will find that in inner stillness you are healed. Here you are at peace. The wrenching loss gives way to a knowing that precedes any verbalization. The secret is to bring that peace into your consciousness and that of others, if possible, as an artist would in the broadest application of that peace. Throw off your inhibitions at self expression, be it in words, sketches, conversation, embraces—and allow that inner calm to be embodied.

Reflection—I have written for years and years. Early in my professional career, intelligence reports were my challenge and delight. Collecting sensitive information from someone who had witnessed or participated in a special meeting and then reporting the information succinctly was especially satisfying. Studying Hemingway's laconic, crisp prose contributed to the skills of this erstwhile intelligence officer. I have also written poetry and as I mentioned previously, kept a journal to record insights and thoughts on the *mystery of life and relationships*, wrote a novel of my CIA experiences, and recently completed an outrageous satire on the greed of an imaginary kingdom in The Middle East, *House of Sand*, drawn from experiences in Saudi Arabia.

When I look back on past efforts to record inspiration, they pale as I measure the inspiration that fires me now. It is as if the grieving process opened a channel to my heart that awaits expression in words, actions, and gestures. Not a day goes by when I do not think gently of Donna and our love—and our continuing love. But this same day also contains such emotions as acceptance, careful resignation, anticipation of the new dawn, a gentle determination, confidence, and inspiration—a listening of a special kind.

No longer do I experience "writer's block," waiting for the muse to alight on my shoulder. Rather, now I find that quiet reflection comes more easily than previously and I listen, and words follow, as in "Inspiration."

---

61 Tolle, Eckhart. *The Power of Now: A Guide to Spiritual Enlightenment.* Novato, Calif., 1999, 24.

Inspiration

Whom do I hear rustling about in my bones,
At the edge of my fingertips,
In the twist of my neck, or
The rumble of my stomach before dawn?

Where do I meet those pleasant memories,
Reassurances of life and soul connections,
Harmony that spans many lifetimes,
But in listening for Love's inspiration?

How do I explain the serenity of Soul,
Clear of anxiety and fear,
Pulsing in harmony with
Creation—near, far, and seemingly departed?

I hear You—close and loving.

Rule 27 Exercise—How does inspiration for new beginnings enter your life? What can you do to attract spontaneity into your life, recover the youthful enthusiasm that once fueled your dreams? Create a Master Plan for your next week. You might want to include an exercise regimen, an evening reserved to pursue interests long dormant, treating yourself to a luxury that could be as simple as a book purchase. And, most importantly, don't forget to include a service to be rendered to someone in need that you have long neglected.

My Thoughts

My Thoughts

My Thoughts

Rule 28—Be prepared to experience the shift to a parallel path that confounds the linear approach to life.

> *Crack yourself open!*
> *What use is it to continue to hide*
> *Behind your facades and roles?*
> *Why waste your energy playing games?*
> *Isn't it time to cry your tears;*
> *To shout your passion;*
> *To dance like Zorba;*
> *And to let your soul touch*
> *The Soul of the world?.*[62]

Prayer—Tell me more about the parallel path.

Response—In life you more often refer to a crossroad. Instead, consider a parallel path, or so it seems, that requires you to leap across a chasm to reach it. And when you do, you discover that what makes the leap so challenging and filled with faith is that the new path might not be on the linear time from which you just departed. So leaping to such a path requires a heroism and deep trust in the divine alchemy that creates without time and space. You will recognize better the parallel path when looking behind to see where you have traveled. You can all cite examples. Now, though, you are being invited to the comfort of the light for the leap into the past of your future.

Reflection—Just when you feel trapped, an opportunity presents itself to break out into new directions, if you so will—if you can command the courage to do so. I studied Greek drama in a Jesuit high school, and I remember how the Greek tragedians made frequent use of a device referred to as *deus ex machina*[63] to extricate the hero from some impossible dilemma.

At the time, I judged the Greek tragedians harshly for what seemed to be the easy way to resolve a life issue. However, the more I consider this ploy now, the more I believe that *deus ex machina* refers to the parallel paths that are present to us—especially in times of grief—that we can all leap onto or cross over to if we so will.

Before we consider parallel paths, let me share some thoughts about lateral thinking as developed by Edward De Bono in his book *Six Thinking Hats*. For

---

62   Martin, William. *The Sage's Tao Te Ching;* New York: Marlowe and Company, 2000, 36.

63   A Latin expression meaning literally *god from a (stage) machine*. In Greek drama, it refers to a god who resolves the entanglements of the play by his supernatural intervention.

De Bono, lateral thinking is a technique "designed to help the thinker to cut across patterns instead of just following along them."[64] For him, lateral thinking sets the stage for that creative, non-logical leap that defies explanation.

Just as in thinking we can adhere rigidly to a linear path of reasoning, so in life we can choose to follow a path that ends in a dark forest, or we can with faith and confidence leap onto a parallel path that shifts our options for soul development. Parallel paths offer thrilling choices to embrace and enhance our life journey. Think of these paths as lines or ridges, equally spaced across a large ball or globe. Running parallel, they do not intersect but seem to.

It is this illusion—that they appear to intersect—that gives us confidence, even courage or heart, to leap across one line, perhaps two, three, or more lines to a distant line or path, and continue our "walkabout," as the Kalihari Bushman would say. And that is how we break that linear, inductive approach to life. To give you something more to consider, what if these parallel paths are not subject to the same time and space limitations to which we are accustomed?

With the lady that I married for so brief a period after Donna's passing, I used to discuss leaping so many timelines and parallel paths to be together. In retrospect, I realize we were probably referring to the opposites we each represented, rather than truly parallel paths. A parallel path marks a significant and bold departure from what one would have anticipated. And sometimes the parallel path might be one that joins us with those who have already moved to another dimension, as in my poem, "Sunset."

---

64   De Bono, Edward. *Six Thinking Hats*. New York: Little, Brown and Co., 1999, 122.

Sunset

At sunset I notice her hands
In the passing clouds
Extend down to reach
Me earthbound.

With confidence
She spirals
Golden light
About me.

I respond hesitantly—
My love and loss intertwined,

Her swirl continues
With determination,
Prodding this weary
Dervish[65] to dance.

I stir …
There is no separation
In this moment.
No distance.
No silence.
No loneliness.

Just eternity
Measured in the movement
Of this golden sunset
After the rains.

---

65 A member of a mystical Sufi order that enters into an ecstatic state through whirling
in dance.

Rule 28 Exercise—Nowhere are parallel paths more important or rewarding than during the grieving and recovery process. In order to conduct the work of espionage under surveillance you first had to see yourself as those conducting the surveillance observed you. Keep a record of who you are or are becoming for three days.

Jot down those activities that are a part of your routine, the thoughts that seem to recur at unlikely times but regularly, the dreams that you recover when you wake, and those that stir your attention during the day.

Once you have the three days written down, pause and allow life path alternatives to emerge. Do not assign any value as to why such a path might be unreasonable, unlikely, or unachievable.

This exercise begins the process of widening your peripheral vision to take in alternatives that you might have missed if you were too focused, or that you had no reason to consider before your loss. At the conclusion of the exercise, ask yourself what parallel paths are opening for you.

My Thoughts

My Thoughts

My Thoughts

RULES 29-34

This chapter could have been entitled "Welcome!" With any luck—or should I say with blessing and awareness—you are moving along a darkened corridor in a cavern buried deep beneath a mountain. You sense that the incline is more noticeable as you gain altitude, and there before you the path curves to the right and you can just make out a glow in the distance. The light seems to come from torches affixed to the walls. Below each torch, carved into the black granite, are a series of admonitions for you to contemplate.

Rule 29—Anchor—don't wobble—and delight in reducing alternatives.

> *The Lama of the Crystal Monastery appears to be a very happy man, and yet I wonder how he feels about his isolation in the silences of Tsakang, which he has not left in eight years now and, because of his legs, may never leave again. Since Jang-bu seems uncomfortable with the Lama or with himself or perhaps with us, I tell him not to inquire on this point if it seems to him impertinent, but after a moment Jang-bu does so. And this holy man of great directness and simplicity, big white teeth shining, laughs out loud in an infectious way at Jang-bu's question. Indicating his twisted legs without a trace of self-pity or bitterness, as if they belonged to all of us, he casts his arms wide to the sky and snow mountains, the high sun and dancing sheep, and cries, "Of course I am happy here! It's wonderful! Especially when I have no choice!*[66]

Prayer—Is acceptance the message of this paragraph?

Response—Yes, acceptance—and let it become calm acceptance that does not look down in gloom. Recall the monk's smile—a wide grin, actually—showing most assuredly the gold fillings that line his teeth. See how he is anchored to the Himalayan rock. Feel his strength. That is what it means to be resolute and with a smile.

Reflection—Acceptance appears at first to be contradictory to the theme of these Rules, but it isn't. Sometimes we do the "on-the-one-hand," followed by "while on-the-other-hand" to distraction. In 1973, I went on a trek in the Himalayas at the same time that Peter Matthiessen recorded the above thought. His goal was to photograph a snow leopard in Nepal. He wrote about his adventure in *The Snow Leopard* and I simply returned to Delhi with memories of the yellow-gray moonscape view at seventeen thousand feet and of the base camp surrounded by towering mountains.

My poem "Straight Ahead Just Before Me" seeks to describe that building excitement that awaits the reader.

---

66   Mathiessen, Peter. *The Snow Leopard.* New York: Penguin Books, 1978.

Straight Ahead Just Before Me

To allow an unfolding when it's cloudy
Is most exiting even if performed in trepidation—
Bright sun rising absent.

Mind anticipating
Seeks familiar patterns, but
This Way is unchanging.

The guide for hire is
Nimble, wise, and wiry.
He tells stories,

Shares rice beer
To loosen the grip
On Past and Future fears,

And leads through the fog bank,
High above deep gorges
That howl despair.

His voice so clear, so intense
In the rushing wind
Leading to a destination unseen—

Straight ahead just before me.

Exercise 29—As you look back on your life, when did you exhibit determination that might have gone against the majority view. How did it feel being you, demonstrating your individuality? Have you done it since? Make a list of five issues important to you—areas where you must make a decision—even where you have procrastinated. Perhaps these issues concern questions about residence, travel, work, or any other matter that has arisen with the loss of the person dear to you. Imagine yourself as the arthritic monk on the mountain precipice and reduce the number of alternatives to the fewest possible. You might find that making decisions becomes easier in this time of stress. Capture your thought process.

My Thoughts

My Thoughts

My Thoughts

Rule 30—Be mad—and I don't mean angry.

> *Look, one day I had gone to a little village. An old grandfather of ninety was busy planting an almond tree. "What, Granddad!" I exclaimed, "Planting an almond tree?" And he, bent as he was, turned around and said: "My son, I carry on as if I should never die." I replied: "And I carry on as if I was going to die any minute. Which of us was right, boss?"*[67]

Prayer—Who is right?

Response—Of course they are both right. The message, however, for you is that it is not death that invigorates you but life, and you will have it abundantly. The true eccentric who breaks all sorts of social norms and expectations is someone who disdains the very thought of death as an irreparable ending. At times of loss it is so important to be sufficiently mad to contradict the norm. Think in paradox—your loss is your gain, death begets life, sanity yields to holy madness.

Reflection—Zorba the Greek was one of my heroes as I grew to maturity, and his hair has grayed and thinned like mine. We both believe we have not lost much speed running down the beach—but we have—we just run alone now. We both howl in the wind sometimes when no one is about. We seek the impossible dream as our compatriot, Don Quixote,[68] did and does. We both prefer to step in unspoiled sand rather than to follow the tracks of another. We both take responsibility for following our bliss, though it might not suit those who would rule us. As I discovered in engaging grief, a certain madness provides some comic relief.

Here is a poem I wrote in veneration of Zorba.

---

67   Kazantzakis, Nikos. *Zorba The Greek*. New York: Simon & Schuster, 1952, 35. Zorba, age sixty-five, is advising the narrator of the story who is thirty-five.

68   Miguel de Cervantes' classic hero Don Quixote, in the book of the same name.

Zorba

Who is that fool with arms outstretched
Above black-haired ankles—pale bare feet?
Whose smile mocks himself no less that those,
Who trudge uphill—dull face to neck.
Why does loose earth remember
His shuffling embrace,
And hum the measured steps
Of the wise?
Does he build bridges?
The column must have begun—now.
Maybe it will end—when?
He has colored it
With his white worn pants
And blue-beached shirt.
His dance is seen and sure for him
Because there is a column.
Your neck is before my face
Because of his madness.

Exercise 30—How "mad"—and I don't mean angry—are you, or are you prepared to be mad now in the self-realization process? Recall five instances where you exhibited *mad* behavior—times where you truly were a free spirit before responsibilities weighed you down. Decide how to rekindle your madness and recover the You who never left your side. Feel the excitement of this challenge. The more committed can check out the classic film *Zorba* with Anthony Quinn and practice your dance steps.

My Thoughts

My Thoughts

My Thoughts

Rule 31—Explore intuitive[69] prayer

> *A new command I give you: Love one another. As I have loved*
> *you, so you must love one another. By this all men will know that*
> *you are my disciples, if you love one another.*[70]

Prayer—Lord, help me to gather in the full dimension of Love.

Response—The full dimension of love is found through loss. And I say this not to have you spend your days in grief over what you no longer have. Love is not something to have, because it is not a thing or a possession. I said *through loss* because it is through loss that time and space no longer have a hold on you. Instead, with the barriers of time and space broken, the full dimension of love descends upon you and you become Love. It is as if—and in reality it *is*—you consume love and you are no longer able to distinguish where you end and Love begins. Consider how your loss in its finality serves for you to recognize and be the love, to share the love that previously was only known in the tasks you performed together or apart. Now you are in a union of Love that invites transparency that knows no boundaries or limits, and is even not exclusive. Loss allows you to comprehend, perhaps for the first time what it means to be in union with me.

Reflection—When I was fourteen years old my mother suggested that I take a summer course in typing to complement my study of Latin and Classical Greek. It did not make much sense to me then, but I can say that I have used and improved this skill over the last fifty years—while I can only mutter a few lines from Xenephon's *Anabasis* and Cicero.

Several years ago, I attended a creative workshop that proved to be a breakthrough for intuitive prayer. Immediately after morning meditation, I sometimes ask a question, or most times just listen and touch-type—eyes closed—what I hear. During the grieving process, intuitive prayer proved essential to my healing. See Appendix E for the fruits of this process as they relate to the Power of Love.

My poem "Golden Chain" recalls the mystery and liturgy of a Catholic service and applies them to life pursuits and self-discovery.

---

69 Intuitive prayer for me is the fruit, the insights, the wisdom, derived from quiet contemplation where I place myself in the presence of the Divine with no other purpose than to listen.

70 John 13:34-35

The Golden Chain

The golden chain swings like a pendulum
The burning incense of ritual prayer—
A faint attempt for union with the Divine.

This morning sways a Soul
An incense bearer conscious,
Yet impatient for return.

The circle spins on—a dervish in prayer
Reminding of past purpose
That outreached grasp,

Or astride a carousel steed
Leaning precariously for brass
Just out of reach.

Is the distance across the lake
Beyond the strength
Of that determined swimmer?

Is Love that calls accepting of those halting steps risking all?
And what of the clean well-lighted place,
Surrounded by comfort, order, and ritual?

Love is discovered when
All is risked for Love.
The adventure of Love is the Power of Love—
I lose You to find you wherever You lead.

Exercise 31—Wake tomorrow early and prepare a quiet place to pray audibly or silently. Have a question for which you seek guidance. When you are sufficiently relaxed and calm, begin your intuitive prayer with the question and record what follows. Read over the results and assess for yourself the value of this exercise.

My Thoughts

My Thoughts

My Thoughts

Rule 32—Celebrate your relationships—Past, Present, and To Come.

> *A good relationship has a pattern like a dance and is built on some of the same rules. The partners do not need to hold on tightly, because they move confidently in the same pattern, intricate but gay and swift and free, like a country dance of Mozart's. To touch heavily would be to arrest the pattern and freeze the movement, to check the endlessly changing beauty of its unfolding. There is no place here for the possessive clutch, the clinging arm, the heavy hand; only the barest touch in passing. Now arm in arm, now face to face, now back to back—it does not matter which. Because they know they are partners moving to the same rhythm, creating a pattern together, and being invisibly nourished by it.[71]*

Prayer—What am I to learn from these words that I came upon without warning?

Response—In one word—trust. Of course, there is a serious element of letting go also. It is in relationship that so many lessons are offered you. Isn't it a shock to learn that you cannot control the feelings of another, control her thoughts and aspirations. You must allow the dance to unfold without setting any timetable for completion, or for that matter, fruition. It is Ego that intrudes its presence, almost by invitation, your invitation. This reading encourages you to learn the dance without the inhibition about what others would think or do. See at a higher level the free flow of love that encircles you as showered upon you by your children, grandchildren, friends, and a special friend, perhaps, who advances closer to share your and her dreams.

Reflection—Upon the marriage of my third daughter, I wrote a reflection on marriage for her and her prospective husband entitled "On Marriage and Trekking in the Himalayas."[72] I sought to compare my experience in marriage to a trek I took to the base camp of Himalayan peak in Western Nepal. When I read the draft to Donna, I remember her wondering how I would tie the two themes together. With the last lines she was satisfied I had.

"Secret Message" captures the enthusiasm and passion for new love.

---

71 Lindbergh, Anne Morrow. *Gift from the Sea;* New York: Pantheon Books, 1997, 104

72 See Appendix D for the full text.

Secret Message

PresenceAttentiveRestfuLness
TimeTOgethertorelaxTendernessCare
CommitmentFaithfulnessStimulatingCreatiVe
DetachmentFreetodanceasonETrustHumor
SimplicityLettinggoResponsivenessAttentionCompatibilitY
COnfidenceGrowthSupportPatienceAcceptanceHonestyPlayfulness
DreamsDeepsharingUnityPhysicalSpiritualSparklingEternalPoeticSpontaneous

Exercise 32—In these last years I have defined relationship as being with some-one who wants to be with me as I do with her. What is relationship for you? Has it changed in these last years, months, or weeks? As Anne Morrow Lindbergh suggests, would you "dance" differently now? Capture your thoughts.

My Thoughts

My Thoughts

My Thoughts

Rule 33—Be Ready to Welcome What You Create or Co-Create

> *... [T]he master of the banquet tasted the water that had been turned into wine ... "Everyone brings out the choice wine first and then the cheaper wine after the guests have had too much to drink; but you have saved the best till now."*[73]

Prayer—Lord, I never took this event seriously. In fact, I wondered to myself why it was even included, especially at the wedding feast Jesus where began his public ministry. Please help me to catch the essential meaning of this recounting.

Response—The wedding feast is clothed in so much symbolism and contains so much meaning, much of it hidden. See how the event reflects Jesus' participation in life, not merely as the bachelor son accompanying his widowed mother. No, Jesus was a full participant where he is the source—note that he is the *source*—of celebration. Instead of letting the event fall flat, Jesus created an atmosphere and a cause for celebration by reinvigorating the feast, just as he reinvigorates your life and gives you cause to celebrate all aspects of your life. He is the capstone that attracts the attention of those around you. Indeed, he led a worthy life; indeed, he conveyed the word—the word of love, the word of forgiveness, the word of compassion, the word of generosity, the word of faith, the word of trust, the word of patience. Do you see now how important this feast of Cana is?

And here is the wine and the water mixing in a divine alchemy and the participants in this feast of love consume it. There is much to contemplate in extracting the rich meaning, much as you extract the fine wine from the grapes. To consider all of the symbols, begin with each noun.

Reflection—So often we ask for guidance or assistance in prayer or in sincere attempts to create opportunities for us. When those opportunities material-ize, we so often fail to recognize them, instead attributing the manifestation to chance, coincidence, or the random nature of life. Is it the Navajos who say there are no coincidences? At least that is what Tony Hillerman[74] writes in his novels set in a Navajo and Hopi environment.

I am reminded of the story of the religious man who is trying to escape a flood. He keeps finding higher ground on which to await the Lord's salvation. When he finally succumbs to the waters and asks plaintively of the Lord why He did not save him, the Lord replies that he sent a rowboat, a helicopter, and so on, but the man was looking for salvation on his terms.

---

73   John 2:9-10

74   The interested reader may see any of Tony Hillerman's widely popular novels featuring Joe Leaphorn and Jim Chee.

Yes, with little preparation—or with a lifetime of preparation—we choose the alternatives in our lives, whether it be new partners to accompany us or how to react to the events in our lives. Grief only heightens our perception of what is transpiring, even if we are the fellow sitting on the roof still awaiting salvation from the rising floodwaters.

"Good Morning" is about rediscovery of love, innocence, honesty—and yes, passion—and all this as at least a respite from what can sometimes be a crushing grief experience.

Good Morning

For the observer,
The one standing aside,
Measuring time and distance, and
Past and future accomplishments,
How fast the weeks pass!

For the lover days and nights,
Hours and minutes,
Laughter and silence in embrace
Do rush by—but in an unmoving Present
With no end in sight or to measure.

Another dawn or sunset is welcomed
In which to luxuriate and explore
With the beloved
In this one, unending moment ...
New dimensions of Soul.

Time does not slow
As much as reach the rhythm
That pulses into union two hearts in bliss.

Exercise 33—But this co-creation, this comingling of soul and body stuff does not end here. A day does not pass that other events do not occur that are consistent with and complement the dreams that you can co-create alone or with another or with the family and friends who show up to be with you. As a youth in the Bronx, I dreamed of traveling the world, and it came to pass. Make a list of what you are co-creating in your life right now—though you might have tucked the dreams behind a cloud. Be a weather-shifter!

My Thoughts

My Thoughts

My Thoughts

Rule 34—And welcome the newborn as the Bearers of Light—and to whom I dedicate this book.

> *One night the boy asked, "What is a prophet?"*
> *"Someone who goes on listening to the same voice he heard as*
> *a child. And still believes in them. In this way he can know the*
> *angels' thoughts."[75]*

Prayer—Is there more you can say about what a child hears?

Response—The biological age of a child is not the issue in this discussion. You should remain a child in the purity, honesty, and directness that distinguish a child, regardless of the years you carry. No need to search through childhood memories to discover when you knew angel thoughts. Listen now and you will hear those thoughts that you have all too readily dismissed as indigestion. Those thoughts go far beyond a moral code of what you should not do, and embrace the love exhibited in what you refer to as *random acts of kindness*. You must note that children do serve as the master practitioners who lead you to the music of the spheres, speeding your recovery of the messages that you might have long-since discarded as not sufficiently mature.

Reflection—Prior to the birth of my first grandchild, I wrote a letter to him and continued the tradition for each of the subsequent eleven children. The theme that emerged over and over again in these notes was one of encouragement, urging them to remember as long as possible the melody of love that they were bringing in with them. Never was a letter more meaningful to me than the letter I wrote to my grandson three weeks before Donna passed. He was born two weeks afterwards.

---

75   Coelho, Paulo. *The Fifth Mountain*. New York: Harper Perennial, 1998, 90.

Dear Light Child:

It is 4 AM and the full moon is lighting the Western sky outside the window of my library. The snow is gone and it is time for you to consider your entry into a world that is anxious to hear your message brought from afar as the people gather in fortresses and bunkers on the eve of war. Do your best to keep that message current as you walk the earth.

Your smile will dispel doubt and bring joy most immediately to Kelley, Liam, and Lander, who have been unable to comprehend the difference you will make in their lives. Each secretly considers you his or her own—but you will quickly reach out to each of them. Your Mom and Dad are eager to embrace you and to share their expansive love with you.

Wow, do you have a story to tell and a life to live that story. It might be too much to ask or expect you to bring peace and harmony to this troubled world, but you will surprise yourself as to the contribution you will make in dispelling darkness and ignorance with a message of love. We are so blessed that you are joining a family that will nurture that message to fruition.

Coming into the world after a long winter, you are probably one who will be seeking the sun. That is OK because your mom has some sunny spots picked out for all of you to visit during any harsh winter. I would not be surprised if the early morning before dawn is your time—and in that, your Dad will be your companion.

Many years ago before your Grammy and Poppy were married, we decided on two inscriptions for our wedding rings. For mine, it is, "The sun also rises;" for Grammy's, "But the night is the longest." As I see the moon descend behind the mountains in the west to make way for the impatient sun to arise, I think of your impatience and await with joy your Dawn.
Love,

Poppy

Exercise 34—What inscription do you wear on your heart? How has it changed since your loss?

My Thoughts

My Thoughts

My Thoughts

RULES 35-39

If you have gotten this far on our journey to *further still,* you might observe your life now as more spiral-deep than linear-flat. With all you have experienced—all the pain, grief, despair, confusion, and loneliness, and even joy and new balance—it might be wise to sit up and fasten your seat belt because you are becoming conscious to the fullness of life that never ceased.

Rule 35—Be open to the bridging experience of New Love.

Your task is not to search for love but to find a portal through which love can enter.[76]

Prayer—In loneliness I have been guilty of searching for love. How can I use the insight contained in those words to influence me in the present?

Response—Searching is ultimately influenced by a desire to control. So these words apply to you and others in that your only responsibility is to trust in God's love for you and his care of you. No need to become anxious about the future of illusion. Rather accept that you are loved. In acceptance, you will find that you open wide a portal through which love can enter quite naturally, actually, quite supernaturally.

Reflection—It was not many days after my loss that I sensed—perhaps inaccurately—the interest of others toward me that went beyond offering solace. Understandably I could not handle even the notion that there would come a time when I could respond to the mature affection and the love of another to accompany me on this journey. But then it happened, and in my initial confusion, I wondered about life, love, death, and my own stability. My loved ones—family and close friends—provided or attempted to provide a buffer to protect me in this vulnerable state—some would define it as a period of acute grieving—where my emotions ran up and down the scale.

But in the end—and I do not mean terminal—I reached a plateau of sorts overlooking the terrain of my life and world. And despite sadness and joy that would sweep over me with regularity, I came to accept what for me became an essential truth—namely, that neither Donna nor I could do anything to affect, good or bad, the beautiful relationship of thirty-nine years that we had experienced.

Many more truths emerged during those months and in fact they continue to surface in my life years later. One of the most startling discoveries for me was to experience firsthand that I—the father of six, the grandfather of ten—could love again. Wow! That is the only word I can use to express the wonder. The poet Juan Ramon Jimenez expressed the same with these lines that I first heard when Donna and I attended a workshop conducted by Angeles Arrien.[77]

---

76   Tolle, Eckhart. *The Power of Now: A Guide to Spiritual Enlightenment.* Novato, Calif.: Namaste Publishing, 2004, 135.

77   See footnote 17 for information on Angeles Arrien.

And she was fifty and I thirty—how could it be that I feel a love I could not explain—ageless, passionate and an eternal fire.[78]

So here I was, wrestling with grief and the stirring of love at the same time, and at times almost overwhelmed by wonder. So personal is the experience that one quickly runs into the reaction of family who are unable to comprehend this force that seems to enfold one in its embrace. And in the process of restoring balance to my life, I encountered a variety of reactions and again received insights more appropriate to this recovery stage.

This experience was not about finding a replacement for the soul-partner who passed on, but rather discovering in another dimension or depth the love I had experienced previously, as in my poem, "Soul Whisper."

---

78   I had recalled that the fellow was late in life and had fallen in love with a much younger woman. So much for my memory as I reveal the biases of my generation of male chauvinists!

Soul Whisper

In the stillness before the gray dawn
When creation rests in wonder and
Listens and feels as the stars tumble
In place and space,

Two lovers soul-whisper in the dark
Learning the language of love
Undiluted by sound, volume, expression.

An open exchange—sometimes simultaneous—
Celebrating the wonder, awe, and
The pulsing energy of love,

Exploring the golden light that flows
Within and between them in tune and harmony
Like those stars and galaxies in flight.

What pleasure to breach the boundaries of
Day and night in the rapture of love
And to return at dawn with that knowing.

Exercise 35—Opening up to new love begins with the calm acceptance the finality of your loved one's passing. Your eyes now have a depth of understanding and a vision we might call wisdom. Look over your landscape and discern the voices you have heard but not seen. Consider now what you want to hear—even in prayer—and what you want to share about the new you who survived for some yet to be defined purpose. Write down your reflections.

My Thoughts

My Thoughts

My Thoughts

Rule 36—See rejection as another aspect of loss and compare the similarities to the grief experience.

> *In rejection the easy flow of the stream of life is denied, is blocked, and rushes in a flood of sadness back over you, forming a whirl-pool of emotion in which you are drawn until you burst to the surface and see the sun rising in the blue sky and all about you is shimmering with life.*[79]

Prayer—Sometimes I feel that I am becoming an expert in understanding the dynamics of rejection—spouse, friend, job, and on and on. What am I to take from the words above?

Response—There is no rejection! Do you disagree? Rejection as you consider it is without basis. The rejection that you think you experience is really your unsuccessful attempt to be someone you are not. If it makes any sense, you are really rejecting that imposter in you. Let me add that you can not be affected by the rejection another displays toward you because you are not seeking approval. Your responsibility is to be who you are without the need to receive endorsement of that truth. Without that need, rejection as you understand it is like bubbles—words from the end of a child's soap dispenser.

Reflection—There are some who grieve over a failed relationship, experiencing a sense of loss almost as traumatic, final, and disorienting as the passing on of a loved one. For those, it is so important to address the sense of loss related to rejection directly, just as we discussed a similar need to face grief and fear directly, if healing is to occur.

Rejection from a failed relationship, especially following the death of a spouse, is similar to an aftershock to acute grief. The sense of loss from rejection is the country-cousin to the loss of a partner through death, and will be even more deadly in challenging your self-worth, emotional balance, and joy of life.

The relationship into which I entered about a year after Donna's death ended amicably—but it ended—within a year. I experienced two major losses in as many years. The insights that I garnered from losing Donna helped me so much in dealing with the failed relationship. It was only when I addressed the rejection issue directly that a certain calm returned to my soul. Especially important for my recovered balance was the discipline and desire to remain in the Present—not to be haunted by the Past, nor mourn inconsolably the loss of a Future dream.

---

79   These words filled my consciousness when I asked about rejection.

It should be no surprise that the same friends and family who provided support in my earlier grief sustained and encouraged me in this travail as well. While I have experienced some loss of physical agility over the years, I must confess that emotionally I am becoming more resilient. Here is a poem that I wrote when it became clear that there was no energy in this relationship.

I wrote "Forgotten Flowers" to respect that mutual dawning of light upon a failed relationship.

Forgotten Flowers

On the last night by chance
She came for dinner
And pulled a stool closer
To observe my preparations.

Relaxed, she sipped a glass of wine
As I iron-grilled the salmon,
Sautéed the butter peas—
I've become so domesticated.

After dinner—Chris now in bed—
She in a chair and I reclining by the fire
On pillows she arranged—I asked
Where is this relationship going?

As I suspected, but could not admit,
The energy was no longer there for her
And yes, she's not able to consider
Again the role of mother.

She seeks unfettered friendship
Without constraints—and I want more,
But received so much from her
In these past, fragile months.

Yet balance is restored
The hidden fear is in the light.
Clarity emerges from the fog—
A beacon for my journey.

I walked her in the snow
To her car on the hill
And held her close
Not realizing she forgot the flowers.

And consider "Fly Fishing" as expressing the difficulty in the final acceptance of rejection, not realizing at the time the value of the lessons brought by rejection.

Fly Fishing

At the bottom of the deep pond
Lush with undergrowth
He swims by instinct—
Fins hardly moving,
Gills subdued in reflection.

Long, dark brown, and solid
He slinks silently
Through the underwater kingdom
Like an attack submarine
In enemy waters.

A ripple above catches his attention—
A fly touch on the surface
Outlined by a late afternoon sun?
He swims upward in a spiral ascent
As a second touch stirs the water.

Then off it goes, reminding him of a winged insect
Sliding across the pond and he moves
Closer still just below the water line
Ready to explode upward
To snatch the tasty morsel.

But then he senses the nasty scar
Along the jaw where a jagged hook
Snagged him and almost pulled him
From his ancient kingdom, and
He became cautious … watchful.

Then he spied an angler wading
In the pond with hip high boots.
With such skill and dexterity
She cast her line here and there
Above him—but unseen he was wiser now.

Is there another reason she called
So late last night, than to practice casting?
Did she seek to lure me to the surface
With her gentle words spoken from afar,
Or is she satisfied to know that I have found peace?

Rule 36 Exercise—If you have experienced loss and rejection, write down the major fears that the rejection stimulated in you and compare them to the fears that the loss of a loved one generated. See the similarities, but at the same time see how you are now more circumspect in considering the experience, and paradoxically more direct.

My Thoughts

My Thoughts

My Thoughts

Rule 37—It's OK to be angry!

> *To be a Person, then, means to have learned the secret and par-*
> *adoxical art: to go out, yet remain within; to exert power, yet*
> *exercise restraint; to transcend, yet remain oneself; to be in move-*
> *ment, yet be in total repose.*[80]

Prayer—Sometimes the words you bring before me seem to present an ideal that I have not yet attained. Guide me.

Response—You are often in movement. Yet after the loss of Donna, you are more balanced than ever before, and this assessment follows four tumultuous, emotion-wrenching years. The beauty of your anger now is that it is not charged with the energy of fear that your anger in the past displayed. We are not talking about the so-called righteous anger. Your anger now is a gentle anger as it relates the woman who left you. Anger, if it remains in the present moment, does not drain you emotionally. Much as a rain squall, such anger passes swiftly through the region of your heart.

Reflection—I remember wondering why I was not angry immediately after Donna passed away—at the fellow who drove into her and Chris, and at God for interrupting our plans. I feared silently that, lacking anger, the healing process would be slowed, or worse, never completed. To those around me, I was most insistent that I had slipped over anger as I healed. And my friends would look at me quizzically. That was my conviction until my second marriage dissolved within one year.

In my rush to recreate an intimate loving relationship—I was confident that the marriage was ordained in heaven—my new wife and her daughter joined Chris and me in the creation of a new blended family. Her inexperience in a long-term relationship coupled with mine in short-term relationships contributed to our inability to adjust to each other.

It took a while—almost six months—for me to experience anger at the rejection. We had agreed on the legal separation with the intention of exploring reconciliation, but her determination to remain five thousand miles apart and rely upon phone calls during which she explained that she was looking for a part-time relationship and a full-time partnership finally stirred the anger that had been missing up until now in the grieving process. The anger yielded in time to forgiveness, compassion, and eventually relief—though a residue of pain still hovers.

---

80 Smith, Cyprian. *Spiritual Life as Taught by Meister Eckhart: The Way of Paradox.* New York: Paulist Press, 1987, 56.

However, no longer do I cringe at the mere mention of divorce. It is still difficult for me to relinquish my sense of failure in this relationship—especially when I take into account what Donna and I weathered during our years together. In fact, I now thank this woman for the special teaching she brought to me. Too soon I had turned from the grieving process for Donna, but in the end the healing process would not be ignored or denied.

The two poems below mark the beginning of a realization and acceptance that my second wife had moved on and it was time for me to do likewise.

"About the Rug" recounts a conversation—one of many with my estranged wife—in which I became aware of how I consciously tried to remain remote, holding my feelings in check—not a comfortable game to master.

In "Darting into Tunnels," my frustration surfaces at her avoidance of serious discussion by claiming she can no longer hear me as she is entering a tunnel.

About the Rug ...

She called this afternoon—her morning—
"The birthday boy is missed"—
"Pity tickets are so expensive
To fly across the ocean."

"How beautiful after the storm," she said,
"A raging stream flows down
To the beach below," and
"The sun ... bright enough to tan."

I keep emotion in check,
Disengagement to sustain,
So recently released
From connected strands of pain.

She called a friend, I hear,
To ship the rug I purchased
For her office—"Sorry,
It now adorns our dining room."

Isn't it interesting to experience once more
Relationship—uncomplicated—
A joy in loving, sharing, praying,
Laughing, dreaming, and creating in the Light.

With you, who once I was, am now—
In anticipation of the dance of love,
An opening to a new dimension
For which I sought in this lifetime.

Thanks for befriending me—

The sun is

    Beginning to

        Shine again.

Darting into Tunnels

Rejection like any loss
Demands attention
So purposeful it is.

Posing as a victim or a saint,
The perpetrator seeks exaltation,
Magnification from the chorus,

Ever shifting she seeks strangers
To pity her plight,
Reciting anew her tale of woe.

Not to be deterred—
Distracted from self-indulgence—
She risks no conversion, no compromise.

When confronted or questioned
With a conflicting truth she darts
As a ground hog into a tunnel of neglect,

Beyond heart-shot,
Where ambition is stoked
Into an arrogance of sorts.

Rejection, like fear and grief,
Demand as much attention from you
As love and forgiveness that transcend all.

Rule 37 Exercise—There is a point in rejection when you must release any emotional cords that still connect you to the relationship just severed. Make a list of the emotional ties that still bind you to your former love, and decide what you must do to be free. You might consider creating a ritual that is meaningful to you—like writing down the ties as you identify them and burning them in a fireplace.

I once gathered up a large box of letters exchanged, poured myself a glass of Irish whiskey, played a CD of Scottish bagpipes, and, with an air of celebration, dispatched the letters to the flames.

It was then that I began to consider this brief encounter as a God-provided diversion from the process of dealing with my grief over Donna's death. Though the diversion—be it pharmaceutical or a failed romance or any temporary distraction—serves a purpose. The grieving process must and will be re-visited until it has fully run its courses.

My Thoughts

My Thoughts

My Thoughts

Rule 38—And what about forgiveness?

Forgive us our trespasses as we forgive those who trespass against us.[81]

Prayer—There's that theme of forgiveness again. Will I ever get it right?

Response—It seems that everyone can define forgiveness and can apply it to how someone else should forgive. The real test, without becoming obsessed, is how to forgive in your heart those who you have injured you. To measure to the highest standard of forgiveness, one must forgive gently, releasing all the fear that was disguised by anger and rejection. Yes, your capacity to forgive is the measure of your capacity to love, words you have heard before, but that challenge you when you are confronted by the stark reality of injury.

Reflection—In any committed relationship I think all would agree that forgiveness is a key element. Forgiveness serves as the catalyst to recommitment on a regular basis. It is the first step toward loving someone. When I was first married, I would like to describe the daily recommitment that Donna and I made each day. More fancifully, in the category of what I would have liked to have done, forgiveness gives us the opportunity to revisit the love commitment we have made and to declare aloud that we still are determined to do everything possible to ensure that the relationship prospers.

In the grieving process it is necessary to honor the forgiveness we extended during our time together and to look how we can now extend that healing grace to others. And do you know, reaching out to others is not that altruistic, because in forgiveness we are healed? It is in forgiving that we are forgiven and healed.

Many years ago, a close friend injured me severely. The experience is so vivid to me yet that I flinch in even recalling the incident. I thought that over time I had made a remarkable recovery and I could have passed a polygraph had I been asked if I had forgiven the trespasser. Quite recently, a close friend, upon hearing of this transgression, suggested that I ask my former friend—with whom I had had no contact in almost forty years—for his forgiveness for my not forgiving him, as it was clear to her that I still nursed wounds from the past. I was overwhelmed by her suggestion.

I tracked down the fellow, left a voice message, and he returned the call days later. When I stated the reason for my call, he and I were both emotionally overcome. We met for lunch a couple of weeks later and both witnessed the fruits of the healing process. "Stealing Zoos" celebrates the power of forgiveness and brings that same energy to the words in the Lord's Prayer. A load whose weight I had disguised for years had been lifted.

---

81 Luke 11:4

Stealing Zoos

I stole into the zoo last night,
Unlocked the cage
To a mighty beast
Confined for thirty years.

He was jet black
With a greasy peppered coat,
Eyes so dark, if not bloodshot
I would have missed their intensity.

It took some boldness on my part
To prod him into the moonlight
Long vicious teeth
Sought to keep me at bay.

I persisted stubbornly—
And with determination
Amid his wailing, gnashing, hissing,
Snapping, feints, and lunges.

Outside the shadow corners of my soul,
He seemed listless, and
Sought in vain refuge
In a spacious field of flowers.

Over his massive shoulder
He clutched a ragged, once-bulging sack
To contain the anger, hate, and betrayal
Of a forgotten past.

I pulled tight a cloak of
Love, compassion, and forgiveness,
As he evaporated into
A golden mist of light.

What kept me from stealing
Into the zoo earlier?

Rule 38 Exercise—Identify three people who have caused pain and suffering to you. In a failed relationship, mention your former disappointment or loss. Describe the event or events leading up to the injury. For each, develop a positive action plan to demonstrate clearly a desire to convey forgiveness as a blessing arising from within.

My Thoughts

My Thoughts

My Thoughts

Rule 39—Recognize that Love is behind it all.

Some day, after we have mastered the wind,
The waves, the tides, and gravity,
We shall harness for God the energies of Love.
Then for the second time in the history of the world,
We will have discovered fire.[82]

Prayer—What a challenge! How do I contribute to harnessing the energies of Love?

Response—Before anyone can harness the energy of Love, you must love and not simply be in love. Love reveals itself in the full spectrum of living—from taking a spouse in marriage to letting her go in love; nurturing children and allowing their free path to discover and enact their purpose; consoling friends, that is, listening and witnessing their lives to include their joys and tribulations; and promoting the message of Love, disguised as peace in an ever-widening circle around you into the family, community, nation, and world. That is what harnessing for God the energies of Love means.

Reflection—I stumbled upon this quote in the foreword to Peter Blatty's *The Exorcist* many years ago. Earlier I had read Tielhard de Chardin's *The Phenomenon of Man*. I was attracted to Tielhard because he was a Jesuit. I had come to admire the independence of the Jesuits from whom I had received twelve years of education. Teilhard challenged the established order with creative approaches to scholarship and with his bold assertions.

An ambulance driver and medic during the First World War, he entered the Jesuit order and studied to become an anthropologist in Paris. He later roamed China and discovered the Peking Man. He offered theories of man's evolution that differed from the orthodoxy of the Vatican. He was silenced and obediently accepted censure, retiring to a life of anonymity in upstate New York, far from his native France.

For a moment, consider that Ernest Hemmingway also served as an ambulance driver in that same war. He sought to unravel the mystery of love in his writing, achieving considerably more fame than Teilhard.

So at the conclusion of *Rules For Engaging Grief*, I return to the mystery of love. What is there in a human relationship with another that stays with us so long? Why do we encounter in our dreams, in a familiar sight where we experienced life together, or in a brand of wine that we shared, the smile of our love? Could it be that the Divine gives us a hint of eternity in the relationships we

---

82   de Chardin, Teilhard. *The Phenomenon of Man*. New York: Harper and Row, 1965.

cultivate and pursue in this life—even those that do not last? Perhaps love for another occurs when we also grasp for the first time, or at least at a deeper level, the Divine in terms that we can understand.

But like most of us, we need to miss the love received before we truly appreciate the love present—that which we receive right now, perhaps in a partner, but surely in friends, children, grandchildren—if we are so blessed—and indeed with strangers who are willing to share their journey of love.

In "Still Point" I seek to describe that moment of love that we all experience if we dare.

Still Point

There are times—
You know the times—
When I look into our eyes
And see beyond the stars.

The blue-gray curtain
Flutters open onto your soul
And there you are piercing fire-hot steel,
Love-rock, flowing lava.

It is only in that eternal instant
Without boundaries or definition
That I recognize you from another lifetime,
Or a galaxy long forgotten.

Recognition in your eyes
Not disguised with a smile—
Soul-to-soul direct,
Other body remembrance.

Essential love self-touching
In that moment before the sound and lights
And motion return and the sweep hand
Moves off still point.

Exercise 39—For the concluding exercise, think over how you would harness for God the energies of Love, given the loss that you sustained. Record your thoughts. Incidentally, there are no wrong answers.

My Thoughts

My Thoughts

My Thoughts

Epilogue

He will wipe every tear from their eyes. There will be no more death or mourning or crying or pain, for the old order of things has passed away.[83]

Prayer—Oh, how I have reflected on this scripture, especially during the last four years. Can you provide me deeper insights?

Response—The old order is passing away, though it is difficult to imagine, given the headlines of violence that you read daily. Building upon the honest grief you all have endured from the loss that at times has overpowered you, a new era of compassion is touching you and seeding the fields of violence. Your tears are providing the nourishment, and before long blossoms of uncanny beauty will emerge from the once-frozen turf.

Reflection—When I started identifying the Rules, I was overwrought at times and sought solace, perhaps distance, in exploring the acute grief experienced. I sought to understand the force that was almost overwhelming me like nothing I had experienced earlier.

An early discovery was that the Rules helped to identify what was occurring within me at the deepest level, and in doing so, they helped me to engage grief, and later to engage a new grief through rejection with a newfound confidence.

Why, you might ask, are there thirty-nine Rules? My answer early on was that I liked the number. One day my daughter-in-law asked me how many years I was married. She smiled knowingly when I responded with the number thirty-nine. Further confirmation in the number came when I was discussing the project with some friends. One reminded that under Roman law only thirty-nine lashes were administered to those so condemned for fear that forty lashes would result in death. In an instant I realized that the number was an appropriate reminder that neither I nor the reader would be tested beyond our strength to endure.

THE END

---

83   Revelations 21:4

AND
A NEW BEGINNING

Tracking Common Reactions to Grief

Deep sighing
Stomach distress
Interest in exercise
Increased blood pressure
Muscular tension
Feeling of suffocation
Interest in expanding horizons
Weight and appetite change
Numbness
Loneliness
Periods of euphoria
Guilt
Depression
Helplessness
Anger
Disoriented to time and place
Withdrawn from friends/activities
Forgetful
Crying a lot
Inability to laugh/feel pleasure
Seeking and providing forgiveness
Disbelief that loss happened/is final
Constant thoughts/images of person
Interest in assuming new responsibilities
Loss of spiritual beliefs

Weakness and fatigue
Rapid heartbeat
Loss of appetite
Restlessness
Sleep disturbance
Prayer deeper
Increased illnesses
Neglect of personal
          care/appearance
Confusion
Sadness
Despair
Hopelessness
Feeling of being lost
Peacefulness
Quieter/more reflective
Unable to concentrate
Blameful of self or others
Interest in creative
          arts/expression
Emptiness
Searching for meaning
Acceptance
Interest in work
Increased compassion for
          others

APPENDIX B

Prayer

Prayer. How simple a word. How universal its appeal. Christian, Muslim, Hindu, Shinto, Sufi, Jew, Buddhist, Native American, and most other people conclude that there is a Creator, a Supreme Being, or collections of gods who intervene(s) in the universe and in their lives. Prayer in its broadest application is a response to and an acknowledgement of the Supreme Being. Through prayer, people attempt to interrupt the deity's interference in their lives, redirect or attract His interest, or achieve union with Him.

In prayer, we beg the Supreme Being's assistance to overcome life's daily trials; ask for sustenance to keep us and those around us healthy; request wisdom to deepen our understanding of the life and death experience; beg for solace to comfort us in our grief; ask for happiness to relieve us in times of trial; call for the power to overcome the adversary; seek forgiveness to bring healing to mind and body; and request encouragement on life's journey.

We also pray, perhaps less frequently or intently, to offer praise and thanksgiving to the Supreme Being for the bounty and harmony He promotes. Perhaps, less frequently still, our prayer is the mindless and emotionless state of being through meditation—there, to be present to and in this creative force.

Prayer, in all its varied manifestations and variations, is our assertion of the Creator. We are also revealing an impulse—bringing into consciousness a deep, inexplicable, but wholly natural desire—to be in touch with Him. No one, by virtue of position, wealth, or education, is excluded from the practice of prayer or awareness of the Creator. Indeed, such characteristics, and the activity and pride they sometimes connote, may do more than anything to inhibit the resonance and depth of our prayer, and to dim the inner glow which sparks our prayer—which is sometimes referred to as grace.

Prayer is not limited to the words memorized in youth, though there are times when the heart is so troubled and the mind so distracted that this form of prayer provides the thread leading back to the prayer's inspiration. The repetition of such prayers may also serve to neutralize an over-active mind, which may be more intent on solving life's daily problems than probing the inner recesses of the heart.

We also pray spontaneously as thoughts and emotions prompt us. We can be alone for such prayer or in an intimate, sharing group. Such prayer is marked by our personalized, honest responses to life's tragic, joyful, perplexing events.

Prayer is reaching out, or in, to the Creator. I once believed that it was I who was initiating contact with the Supreme Being, be it through traditional prayer or through meditation. I am now more aware of our unity with Him. The impulse to pray reflects that unity.

Sometimes we "do prayer," and sometimes our prayer is in the aspect of listening—in "being"—as in meditation where we assume the presence of the divinity for Himself. By "doing," we seek to achieve or confirm the line to the Creator. We want reassurance that what we are doing has value; the message is received, the prayer is answered, the presence of the divine is real and God wants our prayers even though He already knows our thoughts because it is then that we are closest to Him.

The active and doing forms of prayer have a time and space dimension that contributes to us reaching outside to the divine entity, which we imagine inaccurately to be apart from us. Time and space, while accurately depicting how our minds work, limit the dynamism and creative energy of our prayer. Time and space connote linear and consecutive-event mind processes. Our prayer need not be so limited.

Sometimes when I pray, I wonder if I am invoking the assistance of the troll in the fairy tale, who lurked in the waters beneath the footbridge, or am I shouting, crying, or laughing into a deep well, hearing only the echo of my soul, as Satan would have me believe.

Yet prayer is so natural. It is like the breath that fills our lungs. It is our dance with the Creator during which we are enriched, entwined, enmeshed, and become one, with and in the divine.

As a nine-year-old I remember being aware of the Creator's presence, and prayer then was the innocent chatter of a child. In high school, prayer was participating in the mystery of the ancient liturgy of the Roman Mass, in saying a rosary and chanting a litany, or following the Stations of the Cross, the symbolic rendering of Christ's journey to Golgotha and his crucifixion. Carved in my memory are the stations, actually wooden tablets with the consecutive scenes depicted, nailed to the trees along a mountain path on the grounds of a spiritual retreat house in upstate New York.

As I grew older still, prayer became the quiet time in a chapel exploring in whispers life and its choices, church attendance, membership in prayer groups, or personal reflection prompted by an insight or a reading which I jotted down in a journal.

Now, I find myself attracted to prayer that more and more resembles that early childlike awareness of the nine-year-old, minus much of the chatter. My awareness of my surroundings has heightened through prayer. Through the meditation which begins my day, I become alert to the Creator's presence which continues all through the day.[84] Following the meditation, the state of being in prayer, I focus my mind-heart on family, friends, and strangers whose plight has come to my attention. Regarding trials and sufferings, I do not prompt the Creator, as I once did, with solutions, but rather accept the harmony, union, and love the Creator represents for me.

I do similarly as I focus on the ills of the universe—civil war, famine, man-made ecological disasters, and the like. I direct my prayer accordingly, again offering no solution, but asking that harmony be restored to the planet. Such prayer is not bounded by intellectual or emotional development, but emerges from the interior reaches of the soul.

I do not limit my prayer to the perceived ills of the universe. I also give thanks for the blessings that surround me, most immediately in family, friends, health, nature, and job. The list grows as I cultivate a perception of the good that envelops me.

Another aspect of prayer is responsive. It is listening to the plights, aspirations, and joys of those around me. While not a textbook definition of prayer, such occasions are genuine community, participatory prayers—individual souls linked in wonder, concern, sorrow, fear, or any of the emotions which our mortal life on earth generates. Such prayer reminds me of the portion of the Catholic Mass, the Prayer of the Faithful, when the prayer or intention is read and the congregation responds, "Lord, hear our prayer." Only now, the prayer becomes personalized. I know and am able to relate to the individual.

Prayer is powerful. When I observe the results from prayer, my first inclination is to attribute the change to chance, circumstances, or fate. This is so whether it be headline news or a quiet restoration of calm in a family racked with its daily chaos. Once I recognize the limits of the rational mind, I notice a sea of interlinking energies flowing through the universe. These energies represent the creative force or Holy Spirit in whose union we exist. Our prayers reflect that union.

Therefore, when I consider the unexpected turn of world events—the dissolution of the Soviet Union; or the unfathomable influence of individuals outside the established power structure, such as a Mahatma Gandhi or a Martin Luther King; or our growing awareness and response to ecological issues, like

---

84   We are urged to pray unceasingly in 1 Thessalonians 5:18

the destruction of rain forests, acid rain, and global warming; or the remission of a fatal disease in someone I know—I seek the cause.

Without a logical explanation available, I conclude that prayer is responsible. Prayer is to harmony as cause is to effect. Harmony flows with and from the Supreme Being. In union with Him, we release inestimable energy through our prayers. The result is the harmony restored and promoted in the universe. And we participate in and share that fulfilling, "becoming" process.

It is because the link between a prayer uttered in silence and the answer to the prayer is impossible to establish beyond doubt that prayer remains mysterious. In the turmoil, confusion, and chaos of this world, can it be that somewhere—nestled between the fourth rib below the heart, behind the forehead, or perhaps not confined by the body at all—resides within all of us union to the Supreme Being?

In prayer we manifest that union; we discover that union; we give birth to that union. Spiritual development is not recovering what was lost—as in the Garden of Eden mythology—but rather becoming conscious of what is and is to be. Prayer is a sign that acknowledges union with the Supreme Being and creative force of the universe.

Later, however, my prayer life took on a chaotic quality, in a sense more spontaneous and varied. For some reason, I am reminded how I sought control as a father, and let go as a grandfather. No longer do I measure output by input, rather I leave it to chance—or is that faith, maybe belief? Everything is on schedule.

APPENDIX C

Sufi Steps Along the Path

1. Remembrance (*Yad Kard*)—The one who willingly decides to embark on this journey (*salik*) needs to concentrate and must at all costs avoid slipping from the spiritual path.

   Confirmed by the imagery of the rope bridge—I was aware of the necessity of proceeding cautiously on the path, one step at a time. Distractions—and there were many—could only lead to disaster.

2. Attentiveness (*Nigah Dasht*)—The *salik* must be aware of the beauty of mind and heart in respect to the whole of creation.

   In the period immediately following my loss the texture and expansiveness of my heart revealed itself to me as I was consoled and received the support and love of so many, and not to go unmentioned the Divine embrace of grace for which there can be no other explanation.

3. Conscious Breathing (*Hosh Dar Dam*)—The *salik* needs to understand that he is breathing, and must come to appreciate each single breath of his life—as breathing represents a form of meditation.

   Even now, each breath I take proclaims life and the Creator's Love. Centering Prayer as practiced by Trappist and Buddhist monks, leads to that same spiritual consciousness.

4. Journey Homeward (*Safar Dar Watan*)—A *salik* is a traveler on earth who is preparing to travel from this world to the world of God—returning to where we originated.

   Yes, I am on the journey home, and this insight still stirs my soul years after Donna departed. I am delighted that I am able to listen to and touch those in front of me, alongside, and behind.

5. Watching the Feet (*Nazar Dar Qadam*)—A *salik* needs to look at his feet while walking—taking each step with the realization that he is getting

closer to home, though he does not know when, how, or why. By looking at the feet, the *salik* comes to understand his destination and does not allow distractions to veil his heart's longing.

Remaining in the Present, I strive not to be anxious about the Future, nor burdened by the Past. I slow so that my footsteps mirror my heart-steps.

6.   Solitude in the Crowd (*Khalwat Dar Anjuman*)—A *salik* needs to respect others by balancing his outward activities with his inward devotion. Tranquility of the inner with the outer elements of life during this journey distinguishes the quality of being. One must be faithful to oneself, not imposing himself on others, and not allowing others to impose themselves upon him. He is a traveler who needs to continue the journey in order to be free.

Never have I felt the quiet solitude I do—alone on a crowded beach.

APPENDIX D

On Marriage and Trekking in the Himalayas

Many years ago, I journeyed with a friend from Delhi, India, to Pokhara, Nepal, for a trek in the Himalayas. We hiked to fifteen thousand feet and then to the base camp of Doulagiri, a towering twenty-five-thousand foot peak in Western Nepal. Reflecting upon the experience now, I find the trek as a symbol of marriage—at least my marriage—and perhaps you will discover similarities in your own unfolding relationship.

In preparation for the trek, I exercised rigorously, increasing my running distance and speed in a wilderness near the President's polo grounds where they worked the ponies not far from the U.S. Embassy compound. I purchased a pair of boots—which I still have—a couple of weeks before our departure and wore them each day to condition my feet to the stiff leather, since I was not sure that the leather would soften sufficiently before our departure.

Our ride in the Land Rover was not uneventful. Though the Indian map indicated that the major highway led directly to the Nepalese border, we discovered otherwise. We reached a river in Northern India and pulled up to a toll station, not to cross a bridge, but to drive onto a raft not much longer than the vehicle. In midstream of the widest of the four rivers we had to cross, the burly riverboat men insisted that we give them more money else we would not reach the other side.

I remember now with a smile the anxiety I felt when I heard my companion shout, "Punch, punch." I was inside the vehicle freeing the wrench of the Land Rover to use as a possible weapon against the extortionists. I rushed back to his side, only to see that he was negotiating the price for access to the other side, *panch* being the Hindi word for five. We paid, but only when we were assured that one payment covered the other streams as well.

In Pokhara, we hired three Tibetan porters, refugees from the 1959 Chinese invasion of Tibet, to carry our food, clothing, and tents. They usually were paid by the day, but since we considered our time limited (I rushed about more at that time in my life) we arranged a flat rate, thus providing an incentive to the Tibetans to lead us up and back sooner.

We set out on a cloudless day from Fish Tail Lodge, situated in the center of a lake, with Doulagiri, resembling a fish tail, towering in the distance. In my inexperience, I thought of a trek as a steady climb up and afterwards a walk down the mountain. I expected the walk up to be hard and the way down easy. Only hours after we departed the lodge did I begin to suspect that reaching our destination was going to take much more time than I had anticipated. We were in a valley heading toward the steep hills, but did not seem to be getting any closer to the massive rock formation of Doulagiri in the distance.

When the path before us began to rise, I received another surprise. Instead of a steady climb, the path dipped back down, surrendering hard-earned altitude to the hills. Up two hundred feet, down a hundred, up another hundred feet, down a hundred and twenty-five, up higher, down lower, and on and on. I would cover a lot more distance during the trek than I had anticipated in studying a map.

A camera which I carried to photograph nature—wild rhododendron trees in bloom, a panoply of greenery, and snow-covered peaks—proved much more sensitive to the Nepalese whom we encountered as we passed through the small villages of ten or so dwellings grasping the high ground. They worked the miracle of cultivation in terraced gardens carved high above the plains, or trudged along the path with bundles braced along their backs and high above their heads in measured steps no beast of burden could endure.

I became aware of how important it was to care for my feet and how oppressed they felt in the new boots. Walking uphill is no more difficult than descending. My friend and I made a good team—he climbed like a mountain goat and I descended with similar sure-footedness. Never did I feel in more need of water to slake my thirst after hours of uninterrupted walking, though the air temperature was not hot. As we climbed to an elevation free of settlements and grazing, I would stand waist-deep in the rushing glacial waters and drink from cupped hands.

And higher and lower and higher we climbed to where the air goes light and you believe that it would not take much to fly, or slide miles down on a glacier field stretched out before you. Immortal though you be, a walk across the glacier tests your mettle. Step by step, following the footprints of your ancestor on this journey, careful not to stray else indeed you will slide miles to the bottom.

Quiet, unruly quiet, and the wind, and the kite birds sailing the breeze. Oh, to fly, you think, and all you hear are footsteps in harmony on the ice.

A figure approaches, descending from above. He is a European and you get set to welcome him and trade words. He is the first that you have encountered since departing days ago. He does not respond to your greetings. Rejection brings anger, and without thought, you are back on the ground and in the world of strife and struggle and competition and … anger. And then a second figure from the hills approaches. He volunteers that they have lost their companion in a crevasse. "He wandered off the path and was no more …" You forgive your unthinking judgment of the one who passed in silence. A shiver rushes through your body, and you stay closer to the path.

Higher you reach and with the lightness of heart you think you hear the chimes of heaven. Is it the wind rushing through the palm branches or rock formations chiseled by the glacier a millennium ago? The sounds grow closer and you wonder if you are experiencing the symptoms of high altitude sickness. You estimate that you are already above twelve thousand feet. And then, over a barren hill in the distance, you see a long caravan of donkeys approaching, each fitted with a battered bell that swings in rhythm and fills the mountains with music. We are on a smugglers' trade route between Tibet, Nepal, and India.

Oh, the weariness you feel as you are four days out and contemplating a return of four days. It is early morning, though you have been walking for hours. You pass a hut and could swear that in the window stood a liter bottle of European beer. You must be hallucinating and you hesitate to mention the vision to your companion. Your thirst overcomes your reserve, and both of you retrace your steps to the dwelling, the window, and the bottle. You negotiate the price. Sitting alongside the path, you share the bottle. No beer since has been more satisfying.

And what of marriage? A journey, not a destination, filled with surprises sometimes measured in ups and downs, exhilarating sights, adventure, a sense of flying, breathless music, companionship, solitude, silence, joy, and always an awareness of a presence deep inside, like the black, granite surface of Doulagiri that stood immobile but observant as we crawled to its base camp.

APPENDIX E

Power of Love

I returned in prayer several days in a row to the theme of the Power of Love. I gathered the following insights as one would golden coins scattered in a field.

The **Power of Love** is a very basic and yet essential force if we are to understand our life purpose, or *personal legend,* as Paulo Coelho would define it.[85]

The **Power of Love** transcends all other energy surges in the universe. It knows no time and space limitations. You can truly love those souls who have passed on or even those you have yet to embrace.

The **Power of Love** precedes and follows your life on earth, but, paradoxically, even mysteriously, is always in the present. It is an all-knowing energy force because it emanates directly and fully in the Divine Presence.

The **Power of Love** swirls around you and within and colors your aura and energy field with majestic light as you prove willing.

The **Power of Love** imbues the receptive soul with energy that is exhibited by all those gifts known as the gifts of the Holy Spirit.

The **Power of Love** is to be shared, spread around to others near and distant. Those that resist its influence and do not gaze at the Presence it represents have chosen to deny the Divine presence in them. It is a conscious decision.

The **Power of Love** is exhibited in the serenity and calm of the soul when faced with inexorable tragedy, in deep grief, in a lover's embrace, and in all manifestations of worship.

The **Power of Love** is transmitted from afar yet is present within. No need to read books on the subject or take workshops.

---

85 Coelho, Paulo. *The Alchemist.* San Francisco: HarperCollins Publishers, 1998, 21.

The **Power of Love** is like the mortar that holds the bricks in place to form the great cathedrals and edifices of praise.

The **Power of Love** is that melody that you refer to in your letters to your yet-unborn grandchildren. It is the melody of your life and each life. No similar melody, but each reflecting the tone of your being, multifarious, and together harmonizes in a chant of love. That is what is described in scripture with the angels and the faithful in constant hymn of praise. All are one in resonating their individual hymn of praise—manifest in the tune (and tone) of the Power of Love.

No need to teach the **Power of Love** as much as to draw the curtain from it, as in pulling the curtain to reveal a stage where the **Power of Love** is manifest in all of your lives. Truly, then, there are no tears and death is truly dismissed as the curtain is pulled.

The **Power of Love** is like a dark, thick energy that moves through the universe. It is not dark in the sense that you fear it, but dark in the sense of powerful and substantial, filling all voids. It is like the dark blood that flows in your veins before light touches it and makes it appear.

The **Power of Love** is the power that sustains you in your most bitter struggle, in your most grievous tragedy, the power that brings you to deep laughter, or to innocence when you are not innocent.

The **Power of Love** represents and manifests joy.

The **Power of Love** is a deep-throated command uttered on a battlefield, calling you to transform this matter into the consciousness of the Creator, again in love.

The **Power of Love** unites all in one union as it strips away ignorance: ignorance of soul presence beneath a strange exterior, uncommon cultural, rugged terrain, inhospitable environment.

The **Power of Love** gifts you with a curiosity and serenity that allows you to take in the full scene of an alien culture to reach a level of compassion with strangers that breaks boundaries long set. Realize the force it is.

The **Power of Love** is not love on a greeting card. Remember, it is the deep, throaty command that rules and will become known and is becoming known. The term **Power of Love** is not chosen lightly.

The **Power of Love** will ease your passage as it keeps you youthful, playful, and commanding.

The **Power of Love** is confident, not doubting, willing, and serious.

The **Power of Love** is engaging in relationships, and in all encounters.

The **Power of Love** is revolutionary and seeks change—no status quo here.

The **Power of Love** flows like a tsunami, reaching new heights against the shore with little warning.

The **Power of Love** is cleansing—washing clean all that went before—and making right all that seemed wrong. It is the true baptism of Spirit.

The **Power of Love** brings Life into matter, and in the process, consecrates and makes matter holy in a union of love.

The **Power of Love** resonates at a deep level and lifts with a rising frequency those around as they can receive.

The **Power of Love** is that melody that you have referred to before to your grandchildren, but you are referring to it only because, uniquely, you can still hear the melody though much has happened to drown out its lure. So deep is the melody within you that you hear it most days.

The **Power of Love** is overwhelming, and blessed are they who are overwhelmed in its wash.

> *God is love, and the one who abides in love abides in God, and*
> *God abides in him.*[86]

---

86   1 John 4:16

978-0-595-47414-1
0-595-47414-4